TAR

SUCCESS

How You Can Become a Successful Entrepreneur, Regardless of Your Background

Don Dwyer

BOB ADAMS, INC.
P U B L I S H E R S
Holbrook, Massachusetts

Published by Bob Adams, Inc.
260 Center Street, Holbrook, MA 02343

ISBN: 1-55850-245-9

Printed in the United States of America.

J   I   H   G   F   E   D   C

This publication is designed to provide accurate and authoritative information with regard to the subject matter covered. It is sold with the understanding that the publisher is not engaged in rendering legal,
accounting, or other professional advice. If legal advice or other expert
assistance is required, the services of a competent professional person
should be sought.
— From a *Declaration of Principles* jointly adopted by a Committee of the
American Bar Association and a Committee of Publishers and Associations

The author advises prospective business owners to seek professional services prior to starting or investing in any business.

COVER DESIGN: Barry Littmann

*This book is available at quantity discounts for bulk purchases.
For information, call 1-800-872-5627.*

Foreword

These are exciting times in which we live. The years that lie
ahead seem fraught with economic and social uncertainty
for most Americans, yet redirecting our focus to a more
global view quickly reminds us of the many opportunities
we frequently take for granted. As we see freedom dawn-
ing in countries formerly obscured by the Iron Curtain,
surely we realize that America remains a beacon of opportunity for all. And perhaps nothing is more central to the
American image than the prospect of owning one's own
business, being one's own boss, and being free to pursue
one's dreams. However, while the desire to shape one's
destiny is strong, many allow themselves to be ruled by
fears and limiting beliefs.

Don Dwyer has dedicated his life to helping people
around the world overcome their fears, make the decision
to own their own business, and use proven tools to achieve
phenomenal corporate and personal success. Because Don
has been a long-time friend of mine and a participant in
my seminars, I am proud to see how well he has utilized
the principles, strategies, and techniques we have shared
to make a measurable difference not only in his life but in
the lives of others. With the consistent application of the
technologies I've developed, as well as the ones he has developed through practical experience, readers will be empowered to break through their limiting fears and ignite
the desire to take control of their own destinies.

I applaud Don's commitment to sharing these life-
changing strategies with you. Make success your target by
reading—and *using*—what you learn in this book!

— *Anthony Robbins*

Acknowledgments

It took a team of dedicated people to make this book a reality. Dr. John Hayes, my friend, public-relations wizard, and chief editor has made developing this book a pleasure. Dan Kennedy deserves my unending gratitude, as does Brandon Toropov, my editor at Bob Adams, Inc.

Nothing of significance happens without your #1 team—your family. The silent patience of my wife, Terry, allows the river of my life to flow with few ripples. My children, Donna, Debbie, Dina, Don, Jr., Doug, Darren, and Robert are my daily inspirations. My grandchildren, Chris, Dani, Jackie, and DJ remind me that life is a process of never-ending discovery. My sons-in-law, Mike, Clint, and Scott, and my daughter-in-law, Mary, remind me that you don't have to be born into a family to be a loving part of it.

To my assistant, Tracy, who always runs interference for me: Thanks for always being there.

And finally, nothing happens in our organization without the family of home office associates, licensees, their teams, and every human being who has ever touched my life. You are all the wind beneath my wings.

My life is a constant process of learning and sharing information. It is like breathing. I must do it to live. I have a tremendous amount of gratitude for the many people who have shaped my thinking. I have a special appreciation for the wisdom I have gained from Paul Meyer, Tony Robbins, Dr. Morgan, and my friend, Jim Sirbasku.

And to Rosey Grier for living the principles of loving, caring, and sharing above all. And for teaching me that these principles will always be more important than the tangible things of this world—love ya!

Peace and Plenty,

— Don Dwyer

Contents

1.
Do It!

"Imagine how different life would be if people discovered a system that would ensure their growth and, ultimately, their happiness."

DON DWYER

For most people, the real journey in life is the never-ending search for happiness. We all want to be happy. But what is it to be happy?

To me, it's the fulfilling of our personal needs, whatever those needs may be. Not everyone has the same needs. Some people need to feel good about themselves. Some need to feel satisfied with their work, others with their family, still others with their social lives. Some people need to have fun. Some people need to be financially independent. Some people need a big home. Some people need fancy cars. And so it goes.

However, all human beings share one dynamic need, which is to grow. To paraphrase Edward Drury, all people grow to maturity, level off, and die, unless they have new

No matter what needs you fulfill, if you fail to grow mentally and spiritually, you won't ever find happiness, even if you do grow financially.

enthusiasm, new challenges, and new ideas.

It appears, then, that no matter what needs you fulfill, if you fail to grow mentally and spiritually, you won't ever find happiness, even if you do grow financially. It seems to me that most people don't understand the importance of growing. Moreover, most people don't know how.

I grew up with the belief that hard work is the key to success. But during my adult life, I observed many hard-working people who were on a treadmill going nowhere. That told me that hard work alone is not the key to success. What is? I wanted to know, and so I searched and studied every book that I could find that promised to tell me. Some of these books said that goals are the keys to success. However, according to a study by Success Motivation Institute in Waco, TX, 97 percent of people don't set goals! Why? Because goal-setting is a "win-lose" proposition that often keeps people from becoming successful. We set a goal, we miss the goal, we get discouraged, and ultimately we don't try again.

Other books said that affirmations and visualizations are the keys. I heard people telling themselves, "I'm the best at what I do," but it was obvious they didn't believe it. I saw people with bulletin boards filled with pictures of what they wanted, pictures that served only to remind them of their unfulfilled dreams. As good as affirmations and visualizations may be, they alone were not the answers I sought.

People who are really successful have a strong self-image.

I continued my search for the key to success—the key that could lead to riches and rewards, to financial independence, to business ownership, to a life full of fun. And guess what I discovered! I found out that people who are really successful have a strong self-image. They like themselves! While successful people share other characteristics, this strong self-image is the foundation. Without it, real success doesn't occur.

Successful people, and in particular those who are in business for themselves, form the habit of doing the things failures do not do. In a sentence: Successful people do the uncomfortable things in life. Why? Because it helps them accomplish what they want. Successful people also form the habit of always winning, even when it appears to the rest of the world that they are losing. Donald Trump knows the meaning of these words. In the minds of successful people, they never lose. Like Trump, they experience temporary setbacks, but their self-image tells them that they are winners.

Furthermore, I discovered that successful people have a purpose, a mission so strong that they are catapulted toward their targets. Failures take the path of least resistance and are satisfied with the results of doing the things they like to do. But successful people subject themselves to rough times, even failure, knowing that if they never fail, they never learn, and then they can't possibly succeed.

The person whose self-image doesn't allow for the creation of good habits naturally ends up with bad habits.

Self-image is the key. It produces good habits, which build the foundations of success. The person whose self-image doesn't allow for the creation of good habits naturally ends up with bad habits. And it's difficult to form good habits without first developing a strong self-image.

I've seen business people who could have been successful if only they had gone out and knocked on doors. If only they had told someone about their services or their products. If only they had taken some *action*. But they couldn't, because their poor self-image would not allow them. They didn't know how to form the good habit of knocking on doors.

What a pity they didn't know how to change. No one told them that they could have built a strong self-image a day at a time. Little victories build strong self-images. They could go out and knock on one door. Then knock on ten. And do it every day until they formed the habit of knocking on doors. Would they ever enjoy knocking on doors? Probably not. But they'd do it just to be successful

Building your self-image can make the difference between success and failure in business and success and failure in your life.

You already have a strong self-image? Great! Build it stronger. Self-image is not something that you create once and then keep forever. You add to it (or subtract from it) every day. The stronger your self-image, the better your chance for succeeding in life.

Experts will tell you that self-image is created in childhood. Your parents helped you build a positive or a negative self-image. I agree. But that doesn't mean you're stuck with a poor self-image, if that's what you've got. You can change it. Building your self-image requires that you do what successful people do. Follow their *system*. Want to become a great ballerina? Then follow the system of the great ballerinas. Want to become a great orator? Then follow the system of the great orators.

In the course of searching for the key to success in business, I learned what successful business people do. I discovered their *system* and recorded it for myself (and eventually others) to use. Then I modeled it. My personal business success validates the system.

Imagine how different life would be if people discovered a system that would ensure their growth and, ultimately, their happiness.

This book offers you and every reader that system.

By reading this book you will learn about the emotional roadblocks that keep you from making the decisions that will lead to your financial independence and happiness. One of those decisions is to own your own business. Believe me, individual business ownership offers to those who achieve it the ability to grow personally and financially. I don't know about you, but I can't imagine life without controlling my own destiny. Whenever I've worked for other people they didn't provide the atmosphere for me to grow personally, or, sometimes, financially.

This book will also teach you methods for *removing* the roadblocks that keep you from making the decisions that will lead to your financial independence and happiness. These methods provide a practical and enjoyable system for organizing and planning your life, thus ensuring greater success and happiness.

Most importantly, this book will teach you how to improve your self-image and raise the self-esteem of your associates—your employees, customers, and vendors. By doing so you'll be able to increase your financial income and accelerate your journey to a richer, happier life.

You want to build your self-image so that you can achieve higher and higher levels of success? Then follow these steps, all of which are a part of the system explained in detail in this book.

1. Determine your values in life.
2. Define success and develop your personal mission statement.
3. Plan your targets.
4. Enlist team support.
5. Control the fear of disempowering emotions.
6. Form the habit of doing the things that failures will not do.
7. Use the skills of P.I.P. and TROMF, which you'll learn in this book.
8. Make success a moment-by-moment event, not something that happens in the future.
9. Become a master of communication so you can share your success with others.
10. Treat yourself and others ethically.

It's not enough just to *need* to be successful. Need pushes you only so far, then it stops. You've got to be committed to following the system if you're really going to achieve success, and then continue building on that success. In my opinion it is impossible to fail at achieving a target that you are 100% committed to. Test this statement. Think about it. After a little thought, you will probably agree with me. You know how to be successful some of the time. Now let's learn how to be successful most of the time.

I've committed myself by forming a mission statement that is so exciting it guarantees me a lifetime of work and emotional drive. What's my mission statement? To help people around the world to make the decision to own their own businesses. To teach them the principles of personal and business success so that they and all people they touch will live happier and more successful lives.

That's a challenge! And it keeps me going every day.

If your mission statement is big, you will be big in accomplishing it. Make it emotional, too, because emotion creates motion. You may succeed beyond your fondest hopes and expectations. But you will never succeed beyond the purpose to which you are willing to surrender. And your surrender will not be complete until you make it a habit to follow the system that will build your self-image.

If you commit to following the system revealed in this book, your success—at whatever you want to do—is a foregone conclusion. I've used this system nearly all of my adult life, and I credit it for many successes. I've watched thousands of others, including some who were acknowledged failures, use the system too, and succeed.

Using this system I have developed a business conglomerate that earns millions of dollars a year and affords me a luxurious lifestyle—expensive automobiles, a Texas ranch, exquisite horses, a vacation get-away, and the freedom to do whatever I want, whenever I want to do it. I have a wonderful family and many friends. And I have the most precious gift of all—happiness. That, my friends, is truly the American Dream. And more important than all these tangible rewards is the excitement and fulfillment of helping thousands of people realize their dream of business ownership. I've had the thrill of watching all of these special people grow personally and live happier lives. (What's more, I've been fortunate enough to share this endeavor with my family, with all of us working together as a team.)

My system helps me fulfill my mission. By surrendering to my life's mission, I have become the master of my life. You can become the master of your life, too. That's what this book is all about. It's a step-by-step system for designing and evaluating a successful, happy life.

My most positive weapon for success has been the attitude that happiness in life is found not by sitting in the bleachers waiting for things to happen but by taking action to make things happen. That attitude has programmed my mind to say, again and again, "Do it!" It is that message that keeps me constantly in action. So let's "do it!" Read on, and I will show you how *Target Success* can lead you to a successful, happy life.

ACTION ITEM

How good is your self-image?

Maybe you've never thought about it. It's not something people frequently discuss. I encourage you to think about it now. Do you have a good self-image or a poor self-image? It's all about what you think of yourself.

Rate your self-image on a scale of one to ten, with ten representing a perfect score. If you find it difficult to rate yourself, ask some people who know you to rate you. Also ask them what you can do to improve your self-image.

How does your self-image rate? If you rate your self-image between five and eight, you're in good shape. You've got room to improve, but you're on the right track, and this book can help you immensely.

If you rate your self-image below a three, you'll find this book helpful, but you might also consider seeking professional help.

By the way, if you rate your self-image a ten, you may be correct. Then again, maybe you ought to ask around and see what others think of you!

2.
The Journey

"The Rainbow International story is now legendary in the world of franchising."

"What a thrill it is to live life, of which business is a part."

"I learned that from adversity there sprouts a greater seed of success."

DON DWYER

But wait a moment. By now you're asking yourself, Who is this Don Dwyer? How is he qualified to teach me about a system that will lead to personal and financial growth and, ultimately, to a financially independent, happy life?

Those are fair questions. Let me tell you about myself.

I wasn't the most brilliant kid to enter the American educational system. My earliest recollection about school pictures my mother trying to pry my hands from the iron fence that guarded the mysterious St. Margaret's from the rest of the world. It was mysterious because people dressed in black were in charge. (I couldn't tell whether they were men or women, or even whether they were real.) My mother called them by a strange name: "nuns." I wasn't ready to submit myself to what might be discovered in St. Margaret's.

A street worker came to my mother's rescue. He offered me a nickel if I would go into the school. That, no doubt, was the first indication of what really motivated me. It was not money. It was, instead, the fear of poverty!

My childhood occurred during the Great Depression, a phenomenon that scarred me, as well as most people who lived through it. We knew what it meant to be in need, and I resolved at an early age to avoid poverty. There were no allowances in that childhood. If you wanted some money, you earned it by collecting bottles for refunds, delivering groceries, mowing lawns, and shoveling snow, of which there was plenty in my home state of New York.

In those early days I had a fierce desire for independence. I resented the handouts that my mother gave my older brother and wanted no part of her "family welfare program." I always knew I could make it on my own.

I made it through school and eventually to Hofstra University, with time out for a stint in the service. At Hofstra I needed tuition money, and the only way to get it was to earn it. A fellow student told me about a newspaper route in Brooklyn, New York. If I could buy the route and work it part-time, it would pay my way through college.

At the time I owned a beautiful new Ford convertible, which I had purchased with my savings. I loved that car. But I knew that an education would serve me better in the long run. So I made the supreme sacrifice, sold the car, and bought the business. It was one of the best financial decisions of my life.

By the time I graduated from Hofstra, I was making more money in my own part-time business than what the recruiters who came to campus could offer me to go to work for them full-time! So I went into the newspaper route business full-time instead, building a distribution network in New York that ultimately paid me $2 million in today's dollars. Not bad for a twenty-five-year-old. And not a bad return for my Ford convertible.

I was never willing to live failure for even a minute, because adversity is the greatest teacher in the world.

Now let me tell you, these early years were a process of trial and error. I occasionally tasted success, but I also experienced numerous setbacks. However, I was never willing to live failure for even a minute, because adversity is the greatest teacher in the world.

The newspaper distribution business was actually a franchise for the *New York Daily News*, although no one described it that way at the time. Operating this business gave me great insight into people, and it also taught me about building financial worth. What I liked best about owning the business was that it allowed me to do anything I desired. From then on, I always wanted to be a business owner.

When I sold the business, no one had ever sold a distributorship for the kind of money I got. I sold it to two of my employees, who gave me no money down but paid me every week for ten years. Imagine getting a weekly income for ten years without ever going to work! That's got to make you believe that business ownership is simply the greatest way to live.

Meanwhile, I was on to something bigger, far from home in California. While I was in the newspaper business, I had also gotten involved in the entertainment business. I worked with Neil Diamond and Tommy and Dicky Smothers. To work in the entertainment field full-time I had to be in California, so I moved west.

For several years talent management was an exciting business. But it was never more than modestly profitable. In addition, I was always on the road. And with a wife who was left to raise six children, that wasn't a happy situation. I decided to change careers.

My wife and I attended a business opportunity expo in Anaheim, California, and that's where I discovered the Success Motivation Institute (SMI). The company sold management and motivational materials to business executives through franchisees. It seemed to me that an SMI franchise would be a good, stable opportunity. And besides, it would get me off the road.

So I opened an SMI franchise territory, and if you had known me at the time, you would have predicted by appearance alone that I was sure to fail. I was in the entertainment business, remember, and I looked like I still belonged there. I had hair down to my shoulders. How likely was it that business executives in top companies would listen to me, let alone buy from me? *I* was going to sell *them* motivational materials?

Before entering an office, I visualized two trumpeters on either side of the door announcing my arrival.

Not a problem. Before entering an office, I visualized two trumpeters on either side of the door announcing my arrival. When the office doors opened, I saw a red carpet roll out before me. The executives inside had been waiting there all their lives to hear my story.

Hey, I knew there was a slight possibility that all of this was an exaggeration. But how much resistance do you think those executives could give a guy who had my level of self-confidence? I had already learned that whatever I wanted was available to me if only I believed I could have it.

So what happened? In fewer than twelve months I out-sold every other franchisee in the network, and at that time there were 1,500. I then decided I wanted to be the senior vice president of the company. I would have set my sights on the presidency, but that job belonged to the founder of SMI, and he had no plans to become unemployed.

Now, I had no experience being an executive. I had always worked for myself, so I didn't know what it meant to work for someone else. Besides, the guy who was the senior vice president had been in the job for ten years. It wasn't going to be easy to displace him. Still, I saw that position as the perfect opportunity to learn more about operating a franchise business.

After I broke every one of the company's sales records—some of my records still stand today—I was appointed senior vice president at the home office in Waco, Texas. Almost immediately I discovered that I had been an executive all my working life. I was a person who knew how to get things done through other people. I was a natural leader. People followed me because they sensed that I would break the barriers, and they would break them with me.

I eventually left SMI to go back into my own business. I had been researching business opportunities, looking for my own deal, when I discovered a unique carpet cleaning and dyeing business. Right away I wanted to buy it.

The owner, however, wasn't ready to sell. The harder I tried to buy the business, the more he tried to recruit me to work for him. But I was finished working for other people, and I told him so. I wanted my own business again.

Well, we just couldn't make a deal. Then finally one day, as we sat in a coffee shop in Jacksonville, Florida, I penciled out an opportunity that he couldn't refuse. He would license me to operate his business in thirteen states where he currently had little or no business. He liked it! So I quit my $200,000-a-year job and drove back home in a carpet cleaning van.

Yes, from successful business executive to carpet cleaner. And that was a promotion, in my mind. I was back in business for myself. I didn't need a title to achieve my greatest potential. People with strong self-images know what I mean.

The deal I made with the owner of Guarantee Carpet Cleaning & Dye Co. was a fifty-fifty proposition. However, when the legal agreement arrived for me to sign at my home in Waco, Texas, my partner's lawyers had changed the deal slightly. My partner was going to own fifty-one percent of the business, and I the balance of forty-nine percent. At the time, I didn't think it was a big deal. I would work so hard and make him so much money that we would never have any problems.

And indeed, we were profitably in business together for eight years. In that last year I sent my partner a check for $180,000, his share of the profits. That big number got the better of him, because he arrived in Waco soon thereafter to take the business away from me. As majority owner, he had the legal right to do so. But not the moral right.

It was 1981, and I had two choices. Fight or flight. I chose to fight.

My partner arrived in March of that year with a contingent of lawyers, accountants, and consultants. He fired me, took the bank accounts, and then tried to serve me with a court injunction to keep me from even talking to the franchisees I had recruited and supported during the previous eight years.

This was the worst time of my life. My wife was in the hospital, seriously ill. I had to dodge the sheriff to keep him from serving me with notice of the injunction. For fifteen days I scrambled, until finally everyone agreed to a settlement meeting.

We had been meeting for hours, and now it was 3 a.m. We were all tired and testy. My lawyer, a tough, brilliant guy named Vance Dunnam, and my partner's high-priced Dallas attorneys were ready to exchange blows. We were getting nowhere.

So I turned to my partner's representative—my partner remained in his motel and did not attend the meeting—and said, "If we don't settle this, the lawyers are going to keep us in limbo for months."

He agreed with me. So we cut a deal, subject to my partner's approval. I was willing to give my partner all the assets of the company in return for the opportunity to ask 50 percent of the franchise owners to join me in a new company.

I'm sure my partner didn't expect anyone to switch. So he agreed to the deal. I then selected the most loyal and ethical franchisees—not necessarily the biggest producers—and thirty-eight of them said they would join me in a new company called Rainbow International.

I borrowed $50,000 from my local banker, who gave me what he called a "gut level" loan (which meant that instead of going by the bank's rules he was using his own judgment to make the loan). That loan was the spark that lit the fire of success that would eventually travel throughout the world to develop successful first-time business owners.

The Rainbow International story is now legendary in the world of franchising. We currently have more than two thousand franchises sold in twenty countries. The company is a tribute to the moral conviction of the thirty-eight original franchisees who, like me, believed in doing what was right.

As I developed my business, I began to realize the power of multiplication. Franchising is a way of multiplying your talents and time to make more money. It's a system that will all but guarantee success for those who commit to follow the system.

It becomes obvious to anyone who is a Rainbow International franchise owner that the way to make more money is to add vehicles and territories. In other words, put more vans on the road to increase your capacity to clean and dye a larger volume of carpet within your franchise territory. Then, develop additional territories.

But there was something more that I could do to help these franchise owners multiply faster. I had learned that the most expensive aspect of operating a business is acquiring new customers. The least expensive thing would be to go back to the same customer base time and time again, selling them services. However, customers want their carpets cleaned and dyed only so many times per year.

So I thought, what if my franchisees had more services to offer their customers? What if they could offer a customer more than just carpet cleaning and dyeing? Weren't there other home services they could provide? And if there were, imagine the profits to be earned. If a franchisee's current level of business paid for overhead and provided a profit, any additional business would fall to the bottom line! That's the power of multiplication!

I then started searching for other services my franchisees could offer to their customers. I recalled an earlier conversation with a man who wanted me to buy his bathtub refinishing business. That would be a perfect fit!

The business was called Gnu Tub, and the company logo was a cartoon-style gnu (which is a kind of antelope) sitting in a tub. Bill Stull and Harold Staas had owned the business for twenty years. They were brilliant guys who loved old bathroom fixtures and had learned how to refinish them so they looked new. I remember the day they led me into their showroom of refinished antique fixtures. You would have thought they were showing off a priceless collection of art.

Frankly, I didn't immediately share their enthusiasm about old bathroom fixtures. But then I started asking some questions. I was looking at a 1903 double-shell sink, and I asked how much they had paid for it. The answer was $35. Then I asked how much they would get for a refinished double-shell sink. The answer was $1,200. Now I was excited!

I bought Gnu Tub in 1989 and offered territories to my Rainbow Franchisees, as well as to others who wanted to join our network. Within a couple of years we had sold more than four hundred territories in seven countries. The business, which I renamed Worldwide Refinishing, has grown at a rate of 25 percent a year, and it's the leading franchise business of its kind in the world.

I liked this multiplier effect. Not only did I appreciate what it could do for my franchisees, I liked what it could do for our group, too! The same principles applied to us. I already had a nucleus of franchisees. Acquiring a franchisee is expensive. If our existing franchisees added another service, they didn't raise their base overhead. They already had the office, the secretary, and the accounting expenses, so the only additional overhead was the technician. The bottom-line profit on the additional business was very high. They made more and we made more money—a win-win proposition

With that in mind I went looking for a third business and found Mr. Rooter Corporation, a publicly held company. For the second time in a matter of months I had another multiplier to offer my franchise network. Mr. Rooter has sold more than a hundred franchises in three countries. The best is yet to come!

The principles of multiplication continue working at The Dwyer Group. In fact I use these same principles in every area of my life. I use them to multiply my finances, my spiritual life, my health, and my family life. And as I do, I raise my image of who I am.

What a thrill it is to live life, of which business is a part. The tangible rewards are gratifying and personally motivating. It's a powerful feeling to buy anything you want, whenever you want it, and to be able to do the same for the people you love.

My life revolves around my family and a few close friends. All six of my children are involved in our business. We work hard and we play hard.

I live in a log cabin on a river. In front of my cabin is a sprawling ranch on which I raise champion Spanish horses. I love to get up in the morning and watch those beautiful, proud, affectionate animals romp across the fields without a care in the world. They are truly a reflection of my exuberant, life-affirming world.

And to think that only eleven years ago I had lost it all. The best thing that ever happened to me was getting fired and losing my company in 1981. That was the beginning of discovering who I really am. That's when I learned that from adversity there sprouts a greater seed of success.

I believe the seed of success is in everyone. But it has to be nurtured. Find a way to water it, to fertilize it, and greatness will result. It is my hope that you'll find a bucket of water, and a shot of fertilizer, in the pages that follow.

ACTION ITEM

What do you *really* want to accomplish? Makes no difference what it is. Makes no difference how impossible it may seem to you. Makes no difference whether you're prepared to accomplish it or not. Makes no difference what anyone else would say about your craving for this one desire. Whatever it is, state it. And right now, I want you to describe this desire in writing. State what it is and why you desire it. No one needs to know what you've written. Just do it, and set the paper aside.

3.
Changing Your Anti-Entrepreneurial Conditioning

"You can't make fear go away by denying its existence."

"You're going to experience some mammoth mental transitions."

DON DWYER

You have been taught many fundamentally untrue things in life. And if you're going to succeed in business, and in life, you must recondition yourself.

For example: "Security is a good job with a good company." And, by implication, "You cannot have security if you are in business for yourself."

Plus, "It's impossible for an ordinary, average man or woman to get rich." And, "You need enormous amounts of capital and influential contacts, maybe even extraordinary luck, to succeed in business."

My own life story says that all of these "truths" are lies.

You've got to stop believing them!

Have you ever awakened to a foggy day and watched the sun burn away the fog until, eventually, you could see the details of objects even a mile away with brilliant clarity?

I've sat in airports waiting for the fog to clear, and I've experienced the brilliant clarity that eventually occurs. Unfortunately, many people are too impatient to wait for the brilliant clarity.

It's a shame when that happens to people who begin to think about becoming entrepreneurs and starting businesses of their own. Maybe that's where you are now. You're trying to see the possibilities of entrepreneurship through some dense, stubborn fog, and you're impatient, waiting for the brilliant clarity. Hang in there. You're going to experience some mammoth mental transitions. You can't help the way you've been conditioned.

Your peers, friends, coworkers, neighbors, relatives—all of them are sending you anti-entrepreneurial messages that condition you to think negatively about your future as an entrepreneur.

To begin with, you (with some help from me) are going to have to clear away the fog. It won't dissipate on its own. That fog, which keeps you from seeing the brilliant clarity of your happiness and success, consists of all your past conditioning, plus just about all of your present conditioning. Your peers, friends, coworkers, neighbors, relatives—all of them are sending you anti-entrepreneurial messages that condition you to think negatively about your future as an entrepreneur.

The fog is limiting and restrictive. And before I can help you—or anyone—learn the practical and technical aspects of getting started in a new business and becoming successful in life, I need to show you how to get rid of the fog!

I have great sympathy for the hopeful, frightened, ambitious, worried people who think about starting a business of their own. Assisted by my Executive Team at The Dwyer Group in Waco, Texas, I have counseled thousands of such people and continue to do so each day. It's a challenging process, but I'm happy to say that we have a high rate of success.

Conditioned to play it safe

From the moment the umbilical cord is cut, the conditioning process begins. This process trains a person to think and react to various stimuli in a predetermined manner.

For example, when I say the word stranger, what are your thoughts and reactions? Reverting back to your childhood conditioning, you may immediately think any or all of the following:

- "Danger"
- "Don't talk to strangers"
- "Never get into a car with a stranger"
- "Don't accept candy or gifts from a stranger"

All of this is well and good when you're a child, but how about now, as an adult? Upon seeing the word *stranger*, if you didn't think: "Great! Meeting strangers means meeting new people who can introduce new ideas and opportunities in my life. Meeting strangers is fun" . . . then you've got to be reconditioned.

You can't totally "play it safe" and still start a business of your own.

Try this one. Like most children, you were no doubt told by parents and teachers, "It's always better to play it safe than to be sorry." Hmmm. Now comes the time when you're thinking about leaving your job to start a business of your own. Suddenly you're in conflict. You can't totally "play it safe" and still start a business of your own. Chances are you won't ever start a business until you've been reconditioned to think that calculated risks are necessary and acceptable in business.

Have you ever heard these suggestions?

- Get a good job with a good company.
- Don't bite off more than you can chew.
- The rich get richer while the poor get poorer.
- It takes money to make money.

- Some people are meant to be successful and some are not.
- You'll never make it . . . you don't have what it takes.

All of these statements are examples of the conditioning process—at its worst. Conditioning has much more power and impact than many people realize. And unless deliberately changed, the conditioning that occurred in childhood remains with us for life.

To make matters worse, your current conditioning probably isn't much more helpful. You probably associate with people who are very similar to you. Maybe they grew up with you. They still think it's dangerous to talk to strangers and better to play it safe, and they'll re-enforce these "truths" when they talk to you. Tell them that you're thinking about giving up your steady paycheck and starting a business of your own, and you'll terrify them! They'll quickly tell you that 90 percent of all new businesses fail. (U.S. Department of Commerce figures indicate this is not true, at least for franchise businesses.) And they'll preach to you the virtues of job security. (An illusion!)

Breaking through to recondition yourself is a tough proposition. I won't kid you about that. But it's got to be done. Many people drag their old conditioning with them into a new business and fail because of it. They just never had a chance to succeed. They could never see the brilliant clarity of what life would be like if they succeeded.

The good news, though, is that when you break free of your conditioning, you gain an awesome amount of confidence and power. You build self-image. The sense of capability that results is indescribable, although calling it "fantastic" is a good start!

The breakthrough begins with desire

"There are only two things that keep people out of the free-enterprise way of life," says Robert Tunmire. "Money and fear. Money obstacles are manageable if you get past the fear."

Tunmire was an Army brat and a high-school dropout who was working as a dishwasher when I met him. There was nothing in his background or current circumstances that would lead anyone to point at him and say, "There goes a future business tycoon."

In June of 1975 I hired Robert for one day of odd-job labor. He would help me and one of my associates clean and dye some carpets. I picked him up in my Cadillac and drove him to the job site. Robert had never before sat inside a Cadillac. And that relatively minor event had a major, instant impact on him.

"I sat in that beautiful white Eldorado," recalls Robert, "and thought to myself, 'Hey, a guy could get used to this!' I thought about what I knew about Don Dwyer. He was a successful local businessman and a pleasant guy, and I started wondering what it would be like to have his kind of life."

At the job, Robert helped clean and dye a houseful of carpets. At the time, I was unaware of what was going on in his mind.

Robert says, "I was amazed at how good the carpet looked when we finished with it and how easy it was to do the job. Then, at the end of the day, I was very impressed by how happy the customer was with the work. I said to myself, 'I think I could do this.'"

The spark was lit! In spite of a great deal of limiting conditioning, and no qualifications to be in sales or in business, and no good reason to visualize himself as a successful business person, young, live-for-the-moment Robert Tunmire began thinking about new possibilities. Unexpectedly, he saw something he wanted. And as usually happens when someone sees something he or she really wants, he was just about prepared to move heaven and earth to get it.

It wasn't long before Robert was bugging me for a job as a route manager in my carpet cleaning business. I recruited him. Then it wasn't long before he wanted to own his own business, and he asked for a franchise territory. Where'd he get the money to invest in a business? He convinced his parents to put up all their furniture and their car as collateral for the loan he needed to buy one of my franchises. He then sold his car and his motorcycle to buy a van. And he started in business with only $500 of capital, no customers, and a big lump in his throat.

"I remember sitting down and crying," Robert admits.

"I was so scared at what I had done."

Let's look at what happened. Robert Tunmire was a young guy up to his ears in debt with no money, no education, and nothing much going for him. *Until desire jumped in front of him.* Desire is the sun power that burns away the fog of past and present conditioning. The greater the desire, the hotter the sun power, and the faster the fog disappears. Brilliant clarity!

Robert went on to build a successful franchise, then several franchises. He ultimately sold his businesses, making himself financially independent. Now, at the still-youthful age of thirty-one, Robert Tunmire is President of Mr. Rooter, the third franchise company in The Dwyer Group organization. He is eminently successful . . . and happy.

What does Robert's story have to do with you? It has within it the revelation that you need to act on your ideas. Do it! *Desire is powerful*, more powerful than any conditioning.

Reshuffle the deck

At the beginning of your life you were dealt a certain hand of cards from the deck of life. Whether that first hand was strong or weak is something you could not control. But ever since that first hand was dealt to you, you've had more and more to do with the direction of the game and the way you play it.

As you moved into adulthood, you took the deck into your hands. Now you are in control. Your job is to reshuffle the deck, deal yourself the best hand possible, and play it as wisely as you can. The best card you can possibly hold is the one marked *Desire*.

Is desire a vague, theoretical, ethereal emotion? Or a practical, pragmatic emotion?

It can be either, or both.

To succeed in business and life, however, your desire must be practical and pragmatic, clear, definite, and compelling. Only that kind of desire will carry you past your fears.

Most people don't like to admit their fears. They don't like to say they're afraid. Fear is part of conditioning. During childhood you were probably told, "Don't be afraid of the dark," and "Fear is for little kids, not big kids like you."

That conditioning makes it difficult to admit we're afraid as adults.

But everybody feels afraid when they think about getting into their own business. There's no reason to be ashamed about that. It's nothing to deny. You can't make fear go away by denying its existence. My Executive Team and I have found numerous methods to conquer fear, and we teach people these methods every day.

Driven by desire, you test your limits and discover new strengths

As children, we spent a lot of time testing our limits. We learned to walk by stumbling around and falling over until we got it right. Once we were limited to crawling, but one day, bang! Those limits were gone.

We learned to ride a bike by falling, skinning our knees, and getting back on the bike again. Once we were limited to walking, but one day, bang! Those limits were gone.

Then we learned to drive a car, usually with grinding gears, jerky starts and stops, and possibly a fender-bender or two. Once we were limited in distance by our bicycle, but one day, bang! In our car, those limits were gone, gone gone.

Why did we do all that? Wouldn't it have been easier to stay in our cribs? Or on all fours? Or just walk? Why did we take those chances? Easy. We saw others with greater mobility and freedom. We saw others with more opportunities. And we sought that kind of life as our number-one desire!

Unfortunately, as adults, we tend not to test our limits. Kids test every limit they can, including some that their parents wish they wouldn't. But adults don't test much.

Guess what? Successful people do! People who succeed in business test their limits, sometimes every day. Just as they did when they were kids, they get up and try, and sometimes they fall down and fail. But they get up again. And when they reach one new height, they climb some more. And in doing so, they establish a wonderful, progressive pattern of discovering abilities they never knew they had.

I've learned to break boards with my bare hand.

When it was first suggested to me, I didn't know whether I could do it. In fact, my first attempt at it failed. But desire made me try again, and I succeeded. Now, at my franchise seminars, I teach others to do the same thing. At first the franchisees don't believe they can do it. But when they discover that they can, it changes their perceptions about "possible" versus "impossible." Suddenly, they eliminate some of their fear.

Desire did that for them. It can do it for you, too.

Most authors of the business books I've read seem to agree that the top reasons for new business failures include undercapitalization, inability to get financing, lack of management skills, and undesirable economic conditions. *I vehemently disagree.*

My experience and observations have convinced me that anyone who has sufficient emotional commitment— *desire*—to a clear target somehow gets the money even when it should be impossible to get it, somehow learns the management skills, somehow gets the resources, and somehow overcomes even the worst economic conditions.

Desire propels you into action. Desire is the first step to success.

With desire, there are no insurmountable obstacles. Desire clears the fog. Desire forces reconditioned thinking. Desire propels you into action. Desire is the first step to success.

By now, you understand the causes and sources of your reflex reactions, and how this conditioning limits you. You're also more aware now of what you can do to recondition your thinking, and why that's necessary.

It's important to build up your desire for a better way of life. That desire will force you to test your limits, to discover new abilities, and gradually to build your self-image, the common denominator of successful people.

Now, in the next chapter, let's find out what really makes successful people tick.

TROMF THEORY

Have you ever said to yourself, "I want to be free?"

I frequently ask audiences that question, and I always get a resounding, "Yes!"

Webster's dictionary defines freedom as "the liberation from slavery or restraint, or from the power of another." Most of us are not physically restrained; we are not slaves, except to our own powers and the powers of others with whom we are closely associated.

Most often we feel imprisoned psychologically. We are conditioned to believe we can't do what we would like to do because of rules that we've established or that others have established for us. The only way to remove the shackles that bind us is to change the rules!

The main inhibitor to the feeling of freedom is the habit of blaming others for our inadequacies. Children blame their parents for not sending them to college. Employees blame their bosses for not giving them a promotion. Spouses blame spouses for one thing or another. And so it goes.

But blame merely allows someone else, or some situation, to enslave us emotionally and psychologically. The TROMF Theory says that Taking Responsibility Offers More Freedom. Forget blame. Take responsibility. Do it for a week. Take total responsibility for your actions, for your life. At the end of that week, you will know what it means to feel free!

ACTION ITEM

Review the Thirteen Characteristics of Successful Entrepreneurs:

- Value System
- Family-Oriented
- Work Ethic
- Patriotism
- Spiritual Faith
- Responsible Attitude
- Caring Attitude
- Cautious Attitude
- Contentment
- Money Management Skills
- Students of Life
- Communications
- Positive Self-Image

Which of these characteristics is most prevalent in your life? Select only one, the one you've accomplished better than any of the others. Write that characteristic on a piece of paper. Explain how your actions reflect that characteristic. Then—and this is very important—explain how that characteristic makes

continued on next page

you feel about yourself. What do you think of yourself for reflecting this characteristic? How does it make you a better person?

Then, determine which of these characteristics is most absent from your life. Again, select only one of the thirteen, the one you've least accomplished. It may be the one that you've never even thought of before. Write that characteristic on a piece of paper. Explain why this characteristic isn't a part of your life. Next, explain how the absence of this characteristic makes you feel about yourself. Think of ways that you could begin to incorporate this characteristic in your life, and record those thoughts, too. Finally, take action! Develop and use this characteristic in your life today.

4.
The Success Model

"Whatever stands in the way of your liking yourself—get over it."

"Responsibility manifests itself most visibly in successful entrepreneurs."

DON DWYER

Earl Nightingale once observed that if we didn't have good role models to watch, we could just look at what everybody else was doing and do the opposite, and most of the time we'd be on the right track.

Fortunately, we have got good role models to watch. Sometimes we've really got to look to find them, but they're out there. Some are ordinary everyday folks, maybe a family member or a neighbor. Others could be famous. You might find them in the movie industry, on television, in politics (though not often), at a university, or in business. Good role models are everywhere.

One of the best favors you can do for yourself is to seek out good role models and then "model" them. (See chapter 15 for additional information about modeling.) Do what they do. They've already cut a path to success. Now follow it!

Modeling is a terrific success technique that is used by many people, including, most likely, the role models we

33

choose to watch. Our heroes and heroines didn't make it by chance. They latched on to a method (probably invented by a role model), accomplished it, repeated it time after time, and eventually succeeded almost as if it was second nature. They *learned* to do what they do best by modeling other people.

Sometimes modeling occurs automatically, without thinking about it. Children unconsciously learn certain mannerisms and customs from their parents, teachers, and other role models. A child's bouncy walk was influenced by someone. That child will continue walking with a bounce, even as an adult, until he decides to change that mannerism. Once he's an adult it won't be as easy to change, however.

Adults tend not to learn unconsciously, so it's harder for us. Before we can achieve something—such as success—we've purposely got to study it and practice how to do it. Many people have never been exposed to successful entrepreneurs, or to people who enjoyed wildly successful lives. Thus, they had no role models.

The good news is that it's never too late to learn. Once you understand how the process works, you can begin to take the steps to achieve whatever you desire in life.

As I told you earlier, I've helped thousands of people—most with little experience—get into businesses of their own. I've watched many of these people struggle, learn, change, grow, and ultimately succeed. And yes, I've seen some miserable failures, too.

Out of these experiences I've developed a Success Model that, when followed, helps people succeed in business as well as life in general.

The Success Model has three steps, all of which are discussed in detail throughout the chapters of this book.

1. Discover what's holding you back. No doubt it's your conditioning (see chapters 3 and 13). Analyze what's holding you back, where you are in life's journey; and commit to make some changes that will propel you forward.
2. Clarify your value system (see chapter 7). What's important to you? Once you under-

stand your value system, you can set priorities in your life.

3. Decide which paths you want to follow in your life's journey. Set targets (see chapters 5 and 6). Establish your mission for life (see chapter 17).

While creating this Success Model, I've observed hundreds of people who have used it, mostly my franchisees. Through my observations I've categorized the qualities and characteristics of the most successful franchisees — men and women of every nationality. Without these qualities and characteristics, I don't believe the Success Model works. Therefore, I offer this composite model of the successful entrepreneur and suggest that you emulate it.

Thirteen characteristics of successful entrepreneurs
1. Value system

First and foremost, successful entrepreneurs develop a clear, strong value system. They know right from wrong. They understand what's important to them, and they live accordingly. Money is never as important to them as making money honestly.

2. Family-orientation

Among the values of successful people is family. To paraphrase Barbra Streisand, people need people. Our society is one in which we need human contact, not only to overcome loneliness but to see our success reflected in other people.

The family-oriented entrepreneur sometimes has the advantage of working with family members. All six of my children are involved in our business, and I wouldn't have it any other way. Most of the top entrepreneurs in our organization employ members of their family. In our franchises, husbands and wives frequently work together.

Given the opportunity, the successful entrepreneur will bring family into the business.

Involving family in business life provides a unique

kind of satisfaction. Given the opportunity, the successful entrepreneur will bring family into the business.

Even when family members are not involved in the same business, the successful entrepreneur, male or female, places a high priority on family relationships.

Where family isn't important, success is less likely to occur. In my experience that's true among employees, too. Frankly, when I'm considering hiring people for an important position, I want to meet their spouse and visit them in their home environment. The way they treat their family will tell me a lot about how they'll treat their role in my business, which I consider my extended family.

By the way, swinging singles can be family-oriented, so I don't discount them from the ranks of potential successful entrepreneurs. I've had many of them in my organization!

3. Work ethic

Successful entrepreneurs can't be afraid of working hard. Many of my franchisees will tell you that they never worked harder than in their own businesses. There's less work in being employed than in being the employer. It may be true that the employer enjoys more of the benefits, but the employer also puts in time day and night, including weekends, if necessary. Don't get me wrong. Successful entrepreneurs are not workaholics. They enjoy a balance between hard work and recreation, including time spent with their families.

There's something else to be said about the work ethic that's shared by successful entrepreneurs. It means that the work always gets done right, regardless of the pay. Real satisfaction comes from a job well done. Whether it's cleaning a carpet in one house or handling a job for a major hotel client, my successful franchisees give every job the same commitment.

4. Patriotism

What does patriotism have to do with success in business, or in life? It gives you a higher purpose. It changes your attitude from *me* to *we*. I can tell you that my top franchisees believe in it.

Perhaps my own experience would be helpful to clarify the role of patriotism in the life of a successful entrepreneur. I have always been a patriotic person. I'm very grateful for the American way of life and for the opportunities this life affords me every day. Realizing this, I'm perhaps more optimistic than the nonpatriot. I start off each day with a positive outlook knowing that in America, anything is possible. That attitude helps me see opportunities where others see problems.

Patriotic people are grateful people. They always give something back to the community that supports them. This creates a win-win circle—the more they give, the more they get, so the more they give, and so on.

If you don't understand this, or you don't share my enthusiasm for patriotism, just look at the people of the former Soviet Union and the former East Germany. Look at how they're struggling just to get a glimpse of what we take for granted every day in our lives. That should give you a different perspective on the subject of free enterprise.

Just by living in the United States we enjoy an enormous advantage every morning that we get out of bed. That's worth protecting. And the successful people I know share a profound appreciation for this opportunity.

5. Spiritual faith

I know very successful Catholics, Protestants, New Agers, Jews, Buddhists, and so on. The specific religion doesn't seem to matter. What's important among successful entrepreneurs is that they believe in a higher authority. And they have faith in that authority. Faith provides patience, persistence, confidence, optimism, vision, and even a higher level of physical energy. People of faith simply approach life differently. They have an added source of power that gives them an edge in the world of business.

6. Caring attitude

Successful entrepreneurs don't just go through the motions of life. They care about what they're doing. They put their emotions into everything. They care about their families. They care about their customers. They care about their employees.

Yes, they care about making money and putting profits in the bank. After all, those are two of the fundamental purposes for owning a business. But successful people are heard talking more about how to improve their product or service than about how to make more money.

You can tell a caring person by the way he treats his employees. He's not as interested in getting his employees to work harder as he is in helping his employees grow mentally. If he takes care of his employees, he believes his employees will take better care of his customers.

Nor does a caring person resent employees who go on to bigger and better things. In our organization it's common for employees of franchisees to want to buy their own business. Many do. I'm proud to say that among our successful entrepreneurs it's also common for them to help many of their employees become business owners.

Caring people develop a special rapport with their employees. When you go into an office or a business where the employees are treated like family, you know it immediately.

Caring can be summed up by thinking about giving, not getting. Success is much more likely to come to those who give than to those who get.

7. Responsible attitude

Successful entrepreneurs assume responsibility. You're not likely to hear them say, "Let someone else do it." They know that the buck stops on their desk. No matter what the issue, they face it responsibly. For this reason they pay attention to the basic integrity of relationships with customers, vendors, employees, neighbors, and even their community. I'm sure of this: responsibility manifests itself most visibly in successful entrepreneurs. They make money; they don't make excuses! People who are good at making excuses are never good at making money. Those two skills are mutually exclusive.

8. Cautious attitude

I've never met the "wild-eyed, riverboat-gamblin' risk taker" of entrepreneurial myth. Those types are not among my most successful franchisees—nor, I would guess, are they widely found among successful entrepreneurs in general. The people who rise to the top are indeed risk takers, but their risks are calculated.

At one point in the lives of all prospective successful entrepreneurs there were some important decisions to be

THE SUCCESS MODEL   39

made. First they had to decide whether to get into business at all. Then, having made the decision to go ahead, they had to decide what kind of business they wanted to own and operate.

People usually seek out advisers to help them make these decisions. They gather as much information as possible. Eventually, having made their choice, they take the necessary leap of faith. However, the more successful entrepreneurs leap only after measuring the distance!

They take the same cautious approach in making subsequent decisions as well. Whether it's hiring employees, buying new equipment, launching an expensive marketing campaign, or making any business decision of consequence, the successful entrepreneur thinks it through, seeks advice, gathers and analyzes information, and then acts.

Don't confuse this approach with procrastination. Successful entrepreneurs do not avoid decision making. They study every important decision. They don't jump impulsively. They act deliberately.

9. Contentment

If you were to ask me to describe contented people, I'd tell you that they're happy people. What are happy people? Let me tell you what they are not. Happy people are not worried, stressed out, burned out, easily aggravated, frequently frustrated, gripers, complainers, or negative thinkers.

A happy man is not envious. A happy woman does not mutter, "If only . . . ." You know the kinds of people I'm talking about. They envy their neighbor's house, their brother's car, their friend's job. These people spend their entire lives figuratively leaning against somebody else's fence, lusting after what they imagine is a greener pasture.

Successful entrepreneurs aren't like that at all! They're contented. If they lean against a fence, it's their own, and they gaze appreciatively at their own lush, green pasture.

Successful entrepreneurs love what they're doing. You've probably heard the adage, "Find something to do that you feel so good about that you'd do it even if you weren't being paid." Well, that's not economically practical for most of us. We need money to survive. But why not get paid for doing something that you love? That's partly a matter of selection, partly a matter of developing a happy attitude.

In my experience, self-employed people are healthier, take fewer over-the-counter drugs, and live longer than people who spent their lives as employees. That makes sense to me. In my own brief stint as an employee in a relatively conventional corporate structure, I suffered the consequences of office politics, managerial egos, and assorted nonsense. To me that looked like the fast path to an early grave. Or at least an ulcer. In comparison, calling the shots is pure happiness!

10. Money management skills

The successful entrepreneurs I know weren't born into money. They had to stretch financially just to get into business, and as a result they maintain a cautious attitude about their money.

When I think about good money managers who became successful entrepreneurs, many of my franchisees come to mind. They are people who scrimped and saved to become independent business owners. They borrowed money from other sources, usually not a bank. In some instances they mortgaged their home or other assets. They did what they had to do to get the money they needed. Nearly all of them started out in business with debts.

However—and this is important—because of their cautious money management, they were able to pay off their start-up debts in two to seven years and live pretty much debt-free thereafter. At the very least, even if they now carry some business or personal debt, they are in better control of their finances than people who work nine-to-five jobs.

Successful entrepreneurs are people who learn how to get the money they need, and then how to manage the money once they get it.

It's not the mistakes that shape our destiny. It's the way we respond to the mistakes that makes the difference in our lives.

---

11. Students of life

Successful entrepreneurs are constantly learning . . .

especially from their mistakes. Let me assure you that not everything the successful entrepreneur touches turns to gold. Behind every success story is a long list of mistakes!

I could write a book about the mistakes I've made. However, it's not the mistakes that shape our destiny. It's the way we respond to the mistakes that makes the difference in our lives.

Successful entrepreneurs know there's much to be learned every day. They look forward to the experience. In fact, they get out of bed wondering what they'll discover in the course of the day. If they stumble, they pick themselves up, figure out what went wrong, and then get back on track—sometimes not all in the same day, but eventually.

The important thing is that successful entrepreneurs realize they don't know it all.

12. Communications

Can you think of a business that doesn't involve other people? There may be a few, but as a successful entrepreneur, you're not likely to be involved in any of them.

To succeed in business you need to know how to communicate. That's why the successful entrepreneur knows how to listen first and talk second. Too many people mistakenly believe that communicating is talking. "I told them what I wanted, now why didn't they do it?" They didn't do it because the message wasn't communicated. That is, the message was related, but not received (or heard).

Good communicators listen. They listen to what their customers are saying about the company's products or services. They listen to what their employees are saying about their jobs. And before they respond, they make certain they understand what they're hearing. Once the message is accurately received, and a response has been accurately relayed (meaning that it was accurately heard), communication has occurred.

Good communication (between employer and employees, a business and its customers, a husband and wife, a parent and child, and so on) builds the foundation for successful relationships.

However, communications involves more than speaking and listening. For many years I've studied a discipline called Neuro-Linguistic Programming, or NLP, which I'll discuss in greater detail in chapter 14, The Power of Influence. It has helped me become a more powerful communicator, and I encourage you to learn more about NLP. Several books have been written about the subject, and there are many NLP seminars offered around the country.

Research reported in the *British Journal of Social and Clinical Psychology* shows that only about 7 percent of communication is language, the actual words we use. About 38 percent is the tone of voice we use. And the balance, 55 percent, is physiology, or body language.

Effective communication is a powerful advantage for the successful entrepreneur.

13. Positive self-image

Enough was said in an earlier chapter about the importance of self-image. It should be no surprise, then, that a positive self-image is among the characteristics of successful entrepreneurs.

People who succeed tend to like themselves. But people who do not like themselves will struggle to succeed. Whatever stands in the way of your liking yourself—get over it. Seek help to solve the problem, if necessary. Because it's certain that without a positive self-image, you will not become a successful entrepreneur, or even a successful player in the game of life.

The perfect role model

The Thirteen Characteristics of Successful Entrepreneurs describes the perfect role model for you to copy in your pursuit of success in business and life. These characteristics are all exhibited, to some degree, in the most successful entrepreneurs I know. That's not to say that every successful entrepreneur has perfected all thirteen characteristics and maintains them daily. But hey, who's perfect? We're not supposed to be perfect. And we'll never find, in the same body, one role model who exemplifies each of the characteristics perfectly.

Different people, though, have accomplished all of the characteristics to certain degrees, and they continue targeting their lives toward perfecting these characteristics. Those are the people you want to know. Those are the people to associate with, to seek advice from, to do business with, and to emulate. Get close to them.

By the way, perfecting these characteristics reminds me of the main character in the film *Star Wars*. Luke Skywalker is on a journey to discover the "Force," the power that's within us all. You're on a similar journey, seeking answers to the question of who you are so that you can become the "Jedi Knight" you're meant to be. But be careful. You will always have to protect yourself from the Dark Side, from the Darth Vaders of the world. They'll try to hold you back. They don't want you to use the Force within. But believe me, the Force is there, and I believe you'll use it to change your life.

How the model works . . . from one who knows

Will the success model work? What better proof than to hear from someone who has used the model successfully, not only in a commercial business but in a spiritual business, too!

I hadn't heard from Peter Fritsch for several years. At one time he owned a Rainbow International franchise. But he sold the business and entered the seminary to become an ordained priest in the Episcopal Church. Now he was building a church in Sacramento, California, and he was planning to open a new church every eighteen months, either in the states or overseas. What an ambitious goal! Out of the blue, during the Christmas season of 1991, I received a letter from Peter, which I quote in part:

> Dear Don,
>
> I know this letter may be a shock to your system, after three years of not hearing from me! Hardly a week goes by that I don't think of you and mentally thank you for all you have given me . . .
>
> As you may remember, I sold my franchise in May 1989. The person I sold it to has made a good go of it, and continues to make regular payments to us. This money has helped me finance three years of seminary training. . . .
>
> The realities of goal setting that I learned from you are a novel idea in the Episcopal Church, and have set me apart as a maverick. While most of my graduating classmates are trying hard to find any type of paying jobs in the church, my California diocese has promised me two years of an adequate salary package that will enable me to pour all my energy into building the new church. . . .
>
> I started on this project a year ago. I have been corresponding with men and women who have built large churches like this,

including Dr. Robert Schuller... Recently I have had the opportunity to talk with the National Office of the Episcopal Church which has resources in consultants in church planning and growth. It is a major undertaking, but as Robert Schuller told me, "It's better to shoot too high than too low!"

Don, you have helped me so much in many ways. Let me name a few. First of all, you were the first adult who told me I could do whatever I set my mind to do. Secondly, you helped me see how my faith was in accord with goal-setting and achievement. Thirdly, you taught me, through the franchise, to organize my time and energy, to work for me instead of against me, to work smarter as well as harder! Fourthly, you taught me to dream again, something I had forgotten to do since I was a little kid. Lastly, you taught me to believe in myself, to take joy in being who I am, and stop trying to be something I'm not or never will be.

You and my wife are the primary people who are responsible for patiently teaching me to value myself. . . . I can't ever thank you enough for such a gift of life. . . .

Sincerely yours,
Peter Fritsch

Peter Fritsch is a good example of how to make each of the thirteen characteristics a target in your life. When you do, you, too, should anticipate your success!

ACTION ITEM

What will your life be like five years from now? Think about it. Will it be much the same life as you're living now? Or will it be different? It *can* be different, if you want it to be, and this book will lead you to change it.

But for now, just describe the life you plan to live five years from now. Where will you live? How will you live? What will your spiritual life be like, if it exists at all? Will you drive a car? If so, what kind? How much money will you have in your savings account, or checking account? Who are the people you'll associate with? What will be most important in your life? Think of those questions, and others, and record your answers.

Don't worry about anyone reading this information. It's all private and personal. Just think, and relax, and write.

5.
A Whole New
Entrepreneurial Life

"I was more concerned about achieving my goal than I was in enjoying the experience."

"Your past does not determine your future."

"Goal setting does more harm than good for most people."

DON DWYER

By now you know this is not a start-a-business book full of advice about choosing accountants and bookkeepers, putting together business plans, and getting your taxes paid on time. All of that is important, but it's covered repetitively in literally dozens of self-help business books.

My contribution to your process of going into business has to do with the psychological and emotional transformation from life as an employee to life as an entrepreneur. It is a whole new and very different life.

In earlier chapters I discussed the characteristics of successful entrepreneurs, the conditioning of successful entrepreneurs, and the need to follow a system for success. Those are not new subjects, although you may never have given them much thought before and you have surely never read about them from my perspective before. I hope those earlier chapters got you thinking about your own life and how you might need to structure it to set yourself up to succeed in business, and in life in general.

If the last two chapters made you feel uncomfortable because they forced you to examine your life and look at yourself analytically, that's okay. In this chapter you'll begin to understand how you can take the information you learned about yourself and make it work for you.

But before we can make any more progress, you've got to accept one basic idea. Are you ready?

Your past doesn't determine your future.

Actually, the past *does* determine the future if you believe it does. Look at the average person's car and you can make a good guess about the kind of car that he or she will be driving five years down the road. Look at that person's bank account balance and you can guess, within a few hundred dollars, what the balance will be five years from now. Follow this person around for a day or so and you'll know that person's routine for the next five years. That's the way it is for most people. Life becomes a routine.

But not for you. Not if you believe that the past doesn't determine your future.

Your future is entirely up to you.

In fact, your past can have so little to do with your future that five years from now, your life can be dramatically different from the life you just lived during the past five years. Compare these two lives, hold them up side by side, and your life will look like one of those funny before-and-after weight-loss photo ads. You know, the "before" photo shows someone the size of a house, and the "after" photo shows a shapely, youthful-looking new person. That's how different your two lives will look.

If you want to get serious about succeeding in business, and in life, and you want to own the new entrepreneurial life that this book is all about, then you've got to get rid of the notion that your past controls your future.

Why goals aren't the answer

It will certainly surprise many of you that I am *not* going to "lecture" about setting goals. Actually, I'm going to make what some would call a heretical statement: goal setting does more harm than good for most people.

Many authors and motivational speakers talk about goal setting, supposedly to encourage readers and listeners and to inspire them to reach greater heights in their lives. To me a goal seems like something that's a long way away, and I can't get very excited about that. Like most people, I need immediate gratification in my life.

Moreover, goals can be unattainable. Look at the statistics and you'll see what I mean. Only 2 to 5 percent of our population achieves major success—I'm measuring success by dollars. Big dollars. Now, those 2 to 5 percent are avid goal setters. Obviously they achieve their goals, too.

But what about the 95 to 98 percent that don't achieve major success? Many of them set goals too. But what happened to them? They didn't reach their goals. Obviously they gave up. They probably became frustrated on the long, bumpy road to goal achievement, and they quit.

No, they failed first, and *then* they quit. Oh yes. Goals have a finality about them. You either make the goal or you don't. If you don't, you fail. Then you quit. And what does that do to your self-image?

Like goal-setting, targeting imposes a value system, but targeting provides the flexibility of more than one way to be a winner.

I think almost everything we've ever learned about goal setting sets us up to fail, not succeed. Even worse, the goal setting process leaves us feeling miserable about ourselves when it doesn't work. Set a goal. Fail to make it. Quit. And feel miserable. That's a process that I want to avoid, and I bet you do, too.

Targeting is a win-win proposition

I didn't say that goals aren't important. I said that goal-setting is a win-lose proposition, and I don't like the odds. But I do believe in goals. However, I have developed a different approach to pursuing goals. I call it *targeting*. And it's a win-win proposition.

The difference between targeting and goal-setting

goes beyond semantics. The word *goal* is more than four hundred years old, and its meaning is firmly implanted in our minds. We know that if we hit the goal, we win; if we miss the goal, we lose. And that's a disastrous philosophy. Think for a moment about the Olympics. From around the world, the Olympic games attract the best athletes from each competing country. Anyone who makes it to the Olympics is a champion, wouldn't you agree? But then why do most of the Olympic athletes go home losers? Most of them don't win a medal. And the goal, after all, is the medal! In fact, we hear very little about the poor athletes who merely win a silver or bronze medal. If they're not gold medal winners, they're not likely to go down in any history books. How many silver or bronze medal winners land those lucrative television commercials?

In my mind, all who compete in the Olympics are winners, and they should never think any less of themselves. He should be empowered by his experience. But that's not the way it works where a goal is the primary object.

Turn now to the philosophy of targeting. With a target you can hit the bullseye and score big, but you can also hit the circle closest to the bullseye and still win points. In fact, a person who tries hard again and again might never hit a bullseye, but could still accumulate more points than the person who hit the bullseye once or twice.

The goal-setting process leaves us feeling miserable about ourselves when it doesn't work, and it almost never works.

I think targeting, as opposed to goal-setting, is better suited for the entrepreneurial experience. Like goal-setting, targeting imposes a value system, but unlike goal-setting it provides the flexibility of more than one way to be a winner. Like goal-setting, targeting can be used to set objectives in life, but without the negative stigma. It's an empowering word!

Transformational Vocabulary, a technique advanced in recent years by author Anthony Robbins, holds that certain words affect our senses in different ways. When you hear the word "hamburger" you might begin to salivate because you like hamburgers. But if you're a vegetarian and you hear the word hamburger, you might think of dead meat. The meat lover would feel pleasure, the vegetarian would feel pain.

Another example is the word "frustrated." When people say they are frustrated, they shut down. They feel pain. But if you substitute the word "*fascinated*" for "*frustrated*", the reaction is positive, not negative. People who are fascinated by something, rather than frustrated by it, open themselves up to learn more about the subject.

Well now, think of the word "*goal*." It has a painful connotation. You know that if you don't achieve the goal, you're a failure, and that's painful. As a result, you might never set goals for yourself, and in that event, you're just like the person whose life has become a routine. Five years from now you'll be exactly where you are today.

Substitute the word "*target*" for "*goal*." The word target may even bring a smile to your face because you associate it with fun and pleasure. Think about the last time you went target shooting, or the last time you threw darts. If you missed the target, or the bullseye, what did your mind say to you?

"Try again!"

And you did. You tried again and again (if not personally, you probably at least observed someone else try again and again). Even if you only hit a piece of the target, you told yourself, "Good job. Try again." That process of learning continued until you got better and better at target shooting.

Targeting is a process

The concept of targeting hit me like a thunderbolt several years ago when I attended an Anthony Robbins seminar where pole climbing was part of the program on the Hawaiian island of Maui. Yes, I said pole climbing. Each of us had to climb a fifty-foot pole, like a telephone pole. Then, at the top, we had to stand up, jump off, and try to catch a trapeze bar that was hanging eight feet away in mid-air. The trapeze bar was attached to another nearby pole. I should also tell you that we would each be wearing a safety harness attached to a cord, like Peter Pan.

If we caught the trapeze bar, we could swing until our

arms gave away, at which time we would be lowered safely to the ground. If we missed the trapeze bar, well, we missed part of the fun, but we would still be safely lowered to the ground.

At the time of this seminar I was still a goal-setter, and a successful one, but soon to be reformed. Two weeks before the pole climbing event I set the goal of climbing the pole and catching the trapeze bar. Then I looked at what I would have to do to succeed. I watched other climbers make their attempts, and I noticed that the crucial step was the next-to-last one, when the climber has to get both feet on top of the pole.

Once up there I would have one foot planted on top of the pole and one foot still resting on the top rung of the pole, a distance of several inches from the top. I would have to balance myself on the foot that was resting on the eight-inch circumference of the pole while I pulled my other foot to the top, and manage not to fall. Whew! That was going to be tricky.

I knew I had to practice. Any time I set a goal, I always analyzed the situation to figure out what I had to do to succeed. Then I would practice. And eventually I would succeed.

So during the seminar I went into the nearby woods, found a tree stump that was low to the ground and about as wide as the pole, and I practiced. I practiced for two weeks on the ground until I was sure I could manage that last step.

On the day that I was to climb the pole, I was ready! I was assigned to a group, and we were about to hear a lecture from a pole-climbing coach. He was not only going to give us a pep talk and remind us that we would be safe even if we fell off the pole, but he also planned to talk about how to enjoy the process of climbing the pole and jumping off.

However, I couldn't wait. I had to climb the pole right away. And I did. In fact, I climbed it twice. But both times I got to the top and fell off.

Then the coach came over to me and said, "You're goal directed, aren't you?" I replied, "Yes, how could you tell?" He said it was the way I climbed the pole. "All you wanted to do was get it done; you never enjoyed the process." Then he instructed me to climb the pole slowly while enjoying the beautiful scenery of Hawaii. "Then, when you reach the top," he said, "look out at the beautiful view of the ocean and when you are ready, take three deep breaths and catch the trapeze."

I followed his instructions and was amazed at how easy it was. The lesson learned: The goal is not the important thing, but enjoying the process is.

What a pity it would have been if I had missed this opportunity. Imagine, I was in one of the most exotic vacation spots in the world, and I hardly noticed. I was more concerned about achieving my goal than I was in enjoying the experience. In my case, goal setting wasn't negative. It simply blinded me. It kept me from experiencing life as it was meant to be appreciated.

Targeting is liberating

After that seminar, I realized that even when goal-setting worked, it was limiting. That's when I developed the process of targeting. I've used the process ever since that seminar and I've discovered its liberating powers. I've accomplished some targets in recent years that I would never have even tried as a goal setter.

A quick example. Following the Gulf War of 1991, I wanted to do something to help veterans. Not just the Gulf War veterans but all veterans who had sacrificed to protect our shores. So one day I thought, wouldn't it be terrific if I could convince other franchisors to join me, and together we would help veterans get into their own businesses?

I developed a program called the Veterans Transition Franchise Initiative, now known as VetFran. The idea was that franchisors would either forgive or finance 50 percent of their licensing fees, thus making it less expensive for the veteran who wanted to invest in a franchise. In addition, I wanted the U.S. Government, preferably the Small Business Administration or the Veteran's Administration, to sponsor the program.

Using the targeting model, I said, "It would be worth a lot of trouble to create a program that could help twenty-seven million American veterans. Let's do it!"

As a goal setter, I might have said something quite different. "I'm an entrepreneur. I can't work with government red tape. I don't know anything about the bureaucracy in

Washington, D.C. Plus, I'll have to contact all the franchisors in the United States. That's more paperwork that I don't want to do."

Had I been a goal setter at the time of the Gulf War, I would have missed creating the most significant project of my business career. And twenty-seven million Americans would have missed out on a great opportunity. I expect Vet-Fran will eventually create more independent business owners, and employ more people, than any other program conceived or supported by any department of the U.S. Government. I have been commended by the President of the United States for this project and praised by the U.S. Congress, and I have made friends with countless veterans across the country.

And targeting gave me the vision to make the project a reality.

Targeting is the answer

Targeting is a process to be enjoyed. It's not a do-or-die proposition. It is, instead, a philosophy for achieving success, but without the disadvantages of goal setting. In our entrepreneurial lives, we should set up targets, aim, and shoot. If we hit the bullseye the first time, great, so long as we appreciated the process. If we miss the bullseye, we try again, learning as we do.

Targeting is a fundamental philosophy in this book. Without it, nothing else that I have to offer will matter to you as you attempt to build a new, entrepreneurial life. To help you learn how to target success in your life, I'll present Ten Targeting Techniques in the next chapter.

6.
Ten Targeting Techniques

"Targeting has accelerated my own personal and financial growth, while diminishing stress and tension."

"We ought to celebrate every day! After all, we live in America, the greatest country in the world."

DON DWYER

Throughout my life I have watched competent, talented people fail to make progress in their lives, even though they worked very hard. How could that happen? People who had every right to be successful, more so than I, were floundering, struggling, and sometimes giving up. Upon closer examination, I discovered what was happening.

I have always been driven by compelling objectives, which for the moment we'll call goals. If I set a goal, I was determined to hit it, no matter how difficult, no matter how many times I had to fall down and stand up again to pursue it. I was committed to making every goal. Ever since I was a kid I had set goals for myself, and I knew how to accomplish them. Of course, as I explained in the previous chapter, I was consumed by my goals, so much so that I never really enjoyed the journey of success.

Many of the people I met not only didn't know how to accomplish goals—after all, this wasn't a subject in high school or college — they didn't have the commitment to chase their goals. They found it easy enough to establish a goal, but then they simply didn't know how to analyze the steps that were required to capture it.

It always seemed that a goal was a distance away, requiring more time than most people were willing to commit to it. Sure, they wanted to lose weight, but today, not tomorrow. Yes, they wanted to buy a vacation home, but this summer, not five summers later. Absolutely, they wanted to stop smoking, but they couldn't endure the months of agony. Of course they wanted to finish college, but they didn't have the time.

All good goals take time to accomplish. All require a method to bring them into reality. But this is painful stuff for most people. Most people avoid pain! And that's why the most competent, talented people I knew frequently failed to make progress in their lives.

Once I developed the targeting system, practiced it myself, and taught it to other people in place of goal setting, I immediately saw the benefits.

Targeting has accelerated my own personal and financial growth while diminishing stress and tension.

Targeting has helped many of my employees and franchisees, all of whom are introduced to the system. Take, for example, Rodney Lynch, who joined our organization at seventeen. Rodney comes from a family of hardworking, salt-of-the-earth people. He's never believed that he couldn't do better for himself and his family, yet he needed to be taught how to accomplish his dreams. His progress has been steady ever since he learned the targeting system. He has promoted himself through productivity, beginning with the most menial jobs in our company. Now, at age twenty-five, he's a mid-level manager with his sights set on moving to the top. Every day Rodney re-earns his position in our organization, as is our philosophy, and every day he continues to grow. I have no doubt that he's headed for major responsibilities in our company.

People who adapt the targeting system will live richer, fuller lives, of that I am convinced. They will fulfill their personal needs. In a word, they will be happy.

Here's how you can begin to put the targeting system to work in your life.

1. Describe your targets in writing.

The first step toward accomplishing a target is to make the target your own. The best way to do that is to describe the target on paper. I suggest you use a pencil. That way, you can change your mind easily, erase a target or part of a target, and refocus your thoughts so that your target indeed is something that you desire.

The act of writing is a good way to commit yourself to the target. Once you record the target, it's no longer just a dream, or a whim. It's now a dream with a deadline. There it is, in front of you, black on white. Now all you've got to do is figure out how to make it happen!

2. Think big.

The poet Pamela Vaull Starr said, "Reach high, for stars lie hidden in your soul. Dream deep, for every dream precedes the goal."

When you get ready to record your targets, don't hold back. Think. And dream. Then, write out everything you know about that target. Don't just say, "I will start my own business." Explain why you'll start your own business. What dreams will that fulfill? Describe what kind of business. What it will be like to work in the business. How soon you'll start the business. And so on. Think it through and, as you do, record your ideas. Remember, you're writing with a pencil. You can always change your mind.

3. Set realistic targets.

Think big, but be reasonable when you describe your targets. This is the point at which most people set themselves up for defeat. The world we live in demands instant gratification. We cook in microwave ovens, we read condensed books, we find shortcuts to everything. If we see it today, we want it today. Nothing wrong with that. But it's simply not that easy. Sometimes you've still got to pay your dues.

How about these young people who get out of college and expect someone to pay them a six-figure income, plus give them a company car and an expense account? They don't know anything yet. Granted, they've got a college degree, maybe one of the best money can buy, but until they put their theories to work in the real world, they're not likely to find anyone who's willing to meet their pay-roll demands.

Set realistic targets. If you don't, you're setting yourself up to fail even before you take aim. Exercise some patience at this point. Success is a series of small victories en route to your target dream. Enjoy those small victories. By doing so, you're teaching yourself to win!

4. Make your targets personal.

It was Willa Cather who said, "To fulfill the dreams of one's youth; that is the best that can happen to a man. No worldly success can take the place of that."

If you're like many adults, you've forgotten how to dream.

If you're like many adults, you've forgotten how to dream. I don't mean that you don't dream at night. Everyone does. But you may have forgotten how to dream about yourself, who'd you'd like to be, the places you'd like to visit, the things you'd like to do. If you were criticized for daydreaming as a child, it's no wonder that you don't daydream now. Your value system won't permit it!

Well, you've got to do something about that. You've got to dream. It's the only way to personalize your targets. Otherwise you might just as well pursue someone else's targets, because it's not likely that you're going to succeed.

What do kids do when they dream? They make believe. I love to watch kids play. They visualize all sorts of people doing fantastic things. Kids haven't been conditioned by the word can't. Give them an empty box and watch what happens. It becomes a fort, a doll hospital, a kitchen stove, a doghouse. Whatever they want. Ironically, the imagination of children can lead adults to all sorts of exceptional accomplishments and adventures. That is, until some adult comes along, takes away the box, and grumbles, "Grow up." In other words, "You're having too much fun.

Grow up and be miserable, like me."

Fortunately, I've never allowed an adult to strip me of my imagination. It's still very active. I don't have any special qualifications to say that I should be able to expand my business worldwide. Or to become one of the major independent real estate investors in my community. Or to be a breeder of rare Andalusian horses. Or to drive a Rolls Royce. What gave me the right to all that? Only my imagination. My ability to dream like a child while working like an adult.

So dream! If you need some help, consult my Design Your Life Questions at the end of this chapter. That exercise will get you into the state of daydreaming.

Take as much time as you need to dream about your life as you'd like it to be. Your dreams will introduce you to the new you, a person who has specific needs that must be fulfilled. These needs are your personal targets.

5. State targets in present tense.

On a Hollywood movie set, I once had the opportunity to watch how the mind can make the "unreal" seem real. An actress was playing the role of a disturbed character. Right before my eyes, she transformed herself from the pleasant, gentle person she is in real life into a very believable, frightening, raving maniac. As I watched the performance, it occurred to me that she was demonstrating how the mind can focus on a target and act as if it's real.

We can do that, too! And what a difference it would make in our lives if we could go forward with the confidence that we had already reached our targets. What if we could appreciate and enjoy our home as if it were already our targeted dream house? What if we could close our eyes for a moment and sit in the expensive car that we've targeted to buy in the future? What if we could "act as if" our targets were reality?

Experts tell us that the mind can't tell time. In the mind, the time is now. Future time confuses the mind. So instead of writing your targets in future tense, making them unfulfilled wishes, write them in the present tense, as if they were already fact.

Each major change, each achievement, even each significant possession in my life began with a "twitch" of a thought. It still works that way. I get an idea, focus it into a target, and noodle about how I might get it done. I imagine what it would be like if I had already accomplished the target. I experience the "as if" feelings of that accomplished target. And in no time, that target becomes a top priority in my mind. Not too long after, the target becomes a reality.

Now, the mental incubation period might take a week, a month, even a year or more, but the time between the target becoming a top priority and the accomplishment of the target is always short. Psychologists call this the Dominant Thought Principle, and people who master it are able to conceive new ideas, turn them into targets, and achieve them at a rapid pace.

The more of this you do, the better you get at it, and the easier it is to go through the cycle of the Dominant Thought Principle. Earlier in my career I fumbled around quite a bit trying to get the hang of this system. It took a lot of time to move from idea to target to priority to accomplishment. But nowadays, I run through this cycle many times every month. Zap, zap, zap, zap. Eventually, you'll have the same experience, if you work at it.

For now, record your targets in the present tense (for example, "I am driving a new Lincoln Continental"), and begin to "act as if" they're already reality.

6. Identify targets that challenge you.

"Ah, but a man's reach should exceed his grasp," wrote Robert Browning. "Or what's a heaven for?"

Don't put too much stretch into your targets, but stretch. If you do, you'll build your self-confidence, making it easier to accomplish the next target.

Put a little stretch into your targets. Don't be unrealistic. Don't set targets that you can't achieve. Don't put too much stretch into your targets, but stretch. If you do, you'll build your self-confidence, making it easier to accomplish the next target.

While I said earlier that success is a series of small victories en route to your target dream, if your targets are too easily attained, your mind will lose interest in the victories. A guy says, "My target is to make my house payment every month." To which his mind replies, "Big deal. We've been getting that thing paid somehow every month." And the mind rolls over and dozes off. No stretch.

One of the great benefits of entrepreneurial life is personal growth. Most of the people I know who start and develop their own businesses change dramatically in the process. Their self-esteem soars. Their confidence is bolstered. They get involved in community affairs. They become better parents and spouses. They become more interesting people. It doesn't always happen that way, but it's almost a certainty for those who put some stretch into their targets.

7. State targets in positive terms.

Remember when Flip Wilson said, "What you *see* is what you *get*?" Well in 1937, Dr. Napoleon Hill wrote a book called *Think And Grow Rich*, which said, in effect, "What you *think* is what you *get*." Before Dr. Hill the Bible said, "Ask and it shall be given you," which means, "What you *ask* for is what you *get*." And remember that brash young boxer who ran around boasting, "I am the greatest!" and indeed, he became the greatest of his time, reflecting the power of the positive affirmation, "What you *say* is what you *get*."

All of this suggests that the way we structure our thoughts, speak our thoughts, and act our thoughts determines the speed at which we accomplish our target dreams.

State your targets in positive terms. If you say, "I don't want to be poor anymore," you're reinforcing thoughts of poverty and failure. Instead, say, "I'm wealthy, and every day I'm getting wealthier." Refrain from using the words "don't," "can't," and "never" when you state your targets. And don't include threats in your targets, such as "I'll lose weight, or I'll never love again." Stay positive and you'll accomplish your targets faster.

8. Choose targets that excite you.

"The finest qualities of our characters do not come from trying but from the mysterious and yet most effective capacity to be inspired," said Harry Emerson Fosdick.

How you feel about your targets is important in this process. You've got to be inspired. You've got to have a passion to fulfill your needs. You should therefore set "happy" targets.

Some people would say that it's easy for me to have a passion about what I do. I get up in the morning on a multi-million-dollar ranch, drive to the office in a Rolls Royce, work out of a big office, travel to great destinations, and associate with some of the world's most interesting people. Anyone could get excited about that.

But let me tell you a secret. I was passionate long before I got to the ranch, the Rolls, the fancy office, or the worldwide business enterprises. I was passionate about building the largest newspaper route when I had the lousiest newspaper route. I was passionate about my future when I was sleeping in my car between college classes, with no time to get home. I was passionate about cleaning carpets even when my partner fired me and took the business from me. I was passionate when I started Rainbow International. I am passionate about my life, and about what I can accomplish.

The author and motivational speaker Charlie "Tremendous" Jones, sums it up well when he says, "You've got to get excited about the miserable job you've got before you get a job so good that you ought to be excited about it."

I've never thought of anything I've done as a "miserable job." But some jobs have been a lot more enjoyable than others. Yet, I've learned to be excited about whatever it is I'm doing, knowing that my passion gives me an edge most people just don't understand.

9. Tie rewards to every target.

"The highest reward for man's toil is not what he gets for it but what he becomes by it," said John Ruskin.

While money motivates most of us, what we do with the money is frequently our best reward. I recommend that you sock away a small percentage of your earnings just so you can reward yourself at appropriate times.

When you achieve one of your target dreams, reward yourself in whatever manner you prefer. If dinner at a classy restaurant is your idea of a reward, then do it. If you'd rather buy something for yourself, go ahead. Maybe you'd enjoy doing something for someone else. Whatever it is, celebrate!

It's not a good idea to wait until you accomplish a major target dream, one that requires months or a year or more to reach, before you celebrate. Don't forget all the little victories. Celebrate them, too.

In fact, I think we ought to celebrate every day! After all, we live in the most exciting era in human history. We have unlimited opportunities all around us. We have access to knowledge, information, people, and places.

So celebrate!

10. Make targets, not excuses.

My final targeting technique is simply this: Do it!

"Take time to dream . . . it hitches the soul to the stars," wrote an anonymous author.

Don't procrastinate. Don't make excuses. Take the time to plan your life's targets.

Age is of no consequence. Ray Kroc was fifty-three when he launched McDonald's. Colonel Sanders was sixty-five when he began Kentucky Fried Chicken.

Nor does it matter if you've failed in the past. One of our greatest presidents failed a dozen times or more before he arrived in the White House. Look at his chronology:

Failed in business in 1831.
Defeated for legislature in 1832.
Failed again in business in 1832.
Defeated for Speaker in 1838.
Defeated for elector in 1840.
Defeated for Congress in 1843.
Defeated for Congress in 1848.
Defeated for Senate in 1855.
Defeated for vice president in 1856.
Defeated for Senate in 1858.
Elected president in 1860.

If any man had reason to give up, it was Abraham Lincoln. But imagine how different life would be if he had.

I doubt that you have experienced as many major failures as Lincoln. But if you have, I hope you won't give up dreaming. For as Henry David Thoreau said, "If one advances confidently in the direction of his dreams, and endeavors to live the life which he has imagined, he will meet with a success unexpected in common hours."

Dream. Target. *Do it*!

Design your life questions

The purpose of this exercise is to create a thought process that will help fine-tune your life's design and encourage you to focus on specific targets. If nothing else, the following questions should help you dream!

If you could be anyone you wanted to be, who would you be, and why?

_____

_____

If you could live anywhere in the world, where would it be, and why?

_____

_____

If you could do whatever you wanted to do in life, what would it be, and why?

_____

_____

If you could afford the house of your dreams, what would it look like?

_____

_____

If you could afford the car of your dreams, what would it be?

_____

_____

If you could choose the perfect mate, what would that person be like?

_____

_____

If you could choose the perfect family, what would they be like?

_____

_____

If you had the best possible family life, what would that be like?

_____

_____

If you could live the best possible social life, what would that be like?

_____

_____

If you could know one thing you don't know now, what would that be?

_____

_____

If you could be in terrific physical shape, what would you change about yourself?

_____

_____

If you could be more spiritual, how would you act differently?

_____

_____

If you could select your friends, what would they be like?

_____

_____

If you could earn as much money as you desired, how much money would that be?

_____

_____

If you could have any position in business, what would it be?

_____

_____

Say you won the lottery and had all the money you'd ever need, what would you do?

_____

_____

If you found Aladdin's Lamp and the genie granted you three wishes, what would they be?

_____

_____

What does success mean to you?

_____

_____

Now, go back to each of your answers and ask the following questions:

1. Is it possible to live life the way I would like to?
2. How can I make these dreams come true?
3. Can I achieve these dreams doing what I'm doing now?

Turn your goals into targets

The purpose of this exercise is to help you solidify some targets using the creative thinking that you've done to this point. It's been fun dreaming, but you've got to put together a game plan to make your dreams come true.

First, review the answers to questions in the previous exercise and decide which of those answers you'd like to turn into targets.

Then, list five short-range targets. These are targets that you can accomplish today.

Then, list five long-range targets. Long-range targets may require a week, a month, or longer to accomplish.

It's important to form the habit of targeting, so begin with short-range targets that can provide easy, daily successes. Then, work up to targets that will require a week's or a month's commitment. Only then should you target dreams that will require several months to a year or more to accomplish. Studies have shown that it typically takes twenty-one days to form a habit. So now, commit yourself to forming the habit of targeting.

After you list your targets, short-range and long-range, you should arrange them in priority order, with the most important targets ranking number one.

Now list your targets.

Short-range targets

1. _____
2. _____
3. _____
4. _____
5. _____

Short-range targets in priority order

1. _____
2. _____
3. _____
4. _____
5. _____

Long-range targets

1. _____
2. _____
3. _____
4. _____
5. _____

Long-range targets in priority order

1. _____
2. _____
3. _____
4. _____
5. _____

ACTION ITEM

Begin to implement the targeting process now!

In the chart below, list your first-priority target in column one. Be sure you've made your target as specific as possible.

Then, in column two, list all the obstacles that must be overcome before you can achieve your target dream.

In column three, list solutions that will overcome the obstacles in column two.

Set a target date in column four. Our minds work more efficiently when we set deadlines. The target date is the time that you will devote to accomplishing this specific target dream.

In column five, outline the benefits of achieving your target dream. If the benefits don't outweigh the obstacles, it's not likely that you'll put forth much effort to hit the target. If that's the case, reevaluate the target and the rewards and make some adjustments, if necessary. You may discover that the benefits simply don't justify the sacrifices that you'd have to make to accomplish a particular target.

TARGET PRIORITY	OBSTACLES TO OVERCOME	SOLUTIONS	TARGET DATE	BENEFITS OF HITTING THE TARGET
Owning my own business.	Financing	Personal assets.	Three months.	Unlimited income.
	Spouse's cooperation.	Help from father-in-law.		Control over my time; more time with my family.
	How to find the right business.	Keep my spouse informed.		Building a secure future.
		Invest in *Franchise Opportunities Guide*.		No one can fire me but my customers. More travel.

On the next page is a blank chart for you to photocopy and complete for each of your prioritized target dreams.

TARGET PRIORITY	OBSTACLES TO OVERCOME	SOLUTIONS	TARGET DATE	BENEFITS OF HITTING THE TARGET

7.
Values Nurture Success

"I've come to the conclusion that people look inward and ask the wrong questions. Consequently, they struggle to find the true meaning of their lives—their values."

"What's your most important value?"

DON DWYER

A few years ago, my friend Rosey Grier, the former football star, had an opportunity to make a big chunk of money for a few minutes work doing a television commercial. A major wine manufacturer offered Rosey $75,000 if he would simply walk on camera holding a glass of wine.

Rosey could surely have used the money, as it had been many a year since he played football. But he refused to do the commercial. When I asked him why, he told me, "My appearance would've sent the wrong message to all the kids in the ghetto. It would've told them that it's okay to drink. That's not a message that I want to send to them."

By turning down that television commercial, Rosey Grier validated his value system and received the greater benefit of protecting his image. Not many people would turn down an easy seventy-five grand, but Rosey's value system dictated that he had to. That value system hasn't made Rosey Grier a millionaire, but it has made him one of the most admired men in America, a quality most people consider far more valuable than money.

Throughout my life I have observed the importance of values. I've learned that people who violate good and decent values lower their self-image and diminish their ability to earn large sums of money. Even worse, they lose the greater benefit of building an honorable reputation among their family, business associates, neighbors, and friends.

Some years ago I purchased a valuable piece of real estate in Waco, Texas, and I was faced with the challenge of changing the property's zoning from residential to commercial. The previous owners of the property had tried twice to get the property rezoned, but twice they were turned down because area residents opposed their request. The residents were afraid that once the zoning was changed, someone would build a night club on the spot, and they feared for the safety and tranquility of their neighborhood.

After I bought the property, I visited every neighbor who had a voice in the property's zoning status and guaranteed them that I would build a car wash on the site, if it was rezoned to commercial. I got the zoning changed. The very next day I was offered a $500,000 profit for the property by someone who, I'm sure, would have liked to build a night club. Well, I built a car wash instead, and established my reputation as a man of his word in my community. Eventually, that reputation helped make me a fortune in the real-estate market alone.

Build your future on a solid foundation

I once watched a large, modern office and warehouse complex go up in a new industrial park. Months of work and millions of dollars were invested in the building, and when it was finished it was beautiful.

About eleven months after construction was completed, the building began to break apart. To the horror of everyone involved, it literally broke into pieces and had to be demolished before it fell down on its own.

Now, there was nothing wrong with this building. It

just so happened, through either incredible stupidity or incredible duplicity, that the building was erected over a giant sinkhole! The building was good, but the foundation was weak.

I've seen businesses come apart in a similar fashion. It's a shame to see people go through all the trials and tribulations of building a business, only to see the business collapse on top of a weak foundation.

The strength of a business's foundation depends entirely on the values of the owner and of the people who operate the business. So before you begin to build a business, my advice is first to establish your values. Lay the groundwork for a strong foundation that will support the future success of your business.

I don't spend a lot of time looking into myself analytically, but I've learned that it's useful to understand something of what makes me tick. That means it's important to identify my values and to live my life in a way that supports my value system. What's important to me? Happiness, family, health, wealth, success, personal growth, recognition, and learning. The order varies from day to day. It's fair to say that I'm one of the world's greatest jugglers. I have learned to keep many balls bouncing at one time in order to fulfill as many values at once. But I've also discovered that the more successful I become, the more values I can fulfill at any one time. Knowing these truths about myself motivates me, every day, to become as successful as possible.

Many people shy away from self-evaluation, saying that there's no point to it. I meet many of these people at my seminars and at training programs for my franchisees. And I've come to the conclusion that people don't look inward because they don't understand why it's important, and anyway they don't know how.

I've discovered that most people don't give much organized, concentrated thought to values, or identifying a value system. Instead, they're just running along life's byways, somewhat in harmony with an accumulated hodgepodge of values that was suggested to them by parents, teachers, preachers, and employers. Their value system exists, even if they don't recognize it. It may be an outdated value system. It may be one that worked for them as children or young adults. It may be one that worked for them at an earlier period in their lives. But does it work now?

Look what happens when these people try to go into business for themselves. They're living by someone else's value system, one they never embraced. More than likely it's a value system that won't facilitate the achievement of success in business. So what happens when they start a business? They fail shortly after they get started.

Even if by some circumstance they become successful in business, their value system won't support their success for long. Eventually their business will collapse because the foundation was weak.

You want to succeed in business? Then make sure you know what makes you tick—what motivates you—and then be sure you've structured your life to support your value system.

What are the rules you live by?

When I ask people, "What's your most important value?" they usually say "family."

But so many of them don't live as if family is their most important value. They work seven days a week, ten hours a day. Is that the behavior of a devoted family person? When they're not working, they're playing golf, or sneaking away for the weekend while their children stay at home with a babysitter. Is that the behavior of a devoted family person?

Indeed, family may be *important* to these people, but not *as important* as other values.

If you feel, for example, that being good to your family means you have to provide all the trappings of wealth—private schools, a big home, expensive vacations, etc.—you may feel compelled to work long hours to bring in $100,000 or more a year.

However, on closer look, you may find that you value the trappings of wealth more than you do your family. And that may be good, bad, or in between, depending on how you handle it.

What's more important is that you recognize what you value most. Otherwise, you're going to give yourself, and the people around you, mixed signals. And that will result in loads of frustration. On the one hand, you'll tell your family how much you value them. On the other hand, you'll spend most of your time away from your family while you're trying to make more and more money. Until you make a lot of money, you won't be able to buy the trappings of wealth that you really value. Suddenly you're in a vicious downward spiral, and eventually, something's going to crack.

It's so much better to identify your values upfront. Then you can write yourself a set of operating instructions. By doing so, you'll greatly decrease the levels of frustration that otherwise build up in a lifetime, destroying not only businesses but marriages and families.

How to identify your values & establish your rules

Discovering your values is one of the easiest tasks you'll have to perform on your journey to success. The first step is simply to ask yourself this question: What do I consider most important in my life?

Then list the values. Be specific. Don't overlook the Action Item you completed at the end of chapter 3, when you listed the one thing you most desire to accomplish. That may rate as one of your values, although not necessarily. It may be a condition of one of your values.

How do you recognize your values? Well, simply put, they're the things that are most important in your life. They're the things that make you happy. You can identify them by examining your behavior. How do you spend your time? What do you do with your time? And how do you feel about the way you spend your time?

Many people tell me that family is their most important value. I think that's great. However, when those same people look at how they spend their time, family does not rank first. Therefore, how can it be their most important value? They don't put their family before their business, or their job, or their friends, or their church, etc. Looking at behavior to determine values is a revelation for most people. And it's a worthy exercise. Once we recognize our values, and we can rank them in order of preference, we have an opportunity to achieve the ultimate target: happiness!

So go ahead, list at least five values. Do it now!

Five values

_____

_____

_____

_____

_____

The next step is to prioritize your values. Maybe you did that automatically when you listed them. But if you didn't, prioritize them now.

Top five values

1. _____

2. _____

3. _____

4. _____

5. _____

Describe what has to happen in your life—what expectations need to be met—to validate your values.

Now write the conditions by which each of your top five values will be fulfilled. In other words, describe what has to happen in your life—what expectations need to be met—to validate your values. If happiness is one of your values, what will make you happy? If family is one of your values, what is it about family that fulfills this value for you? Go through this process for each of your top five values. Do it now.

Conditions to validate value #1

1. _____

2. _____

3. _____

4. _____

5. _____

Conditions to validate value #2

1. _____

2. _____

3. _____

4. _____

5. _____

Conditions to validate value #3

1. _____

2. _____

3. _____

4. _____

5. _____

Conditions to validate value #4

1. _____

2. _____

3. _____

4. _____

5. _____

Conditions to validate value #5

1. _____

2. _____

3. _____

4. _____

5. _____

Let's say, for example, that you ranked happiness as

your number-one priority. And to be happy, you said you need to earn $150,000 a year, drive a Rolls Royce, own a vacation home in the Cayman Islands, and only work two days a week. Sounds great, doesn't it?

But if you're twenty-two years old and you've just graduated from college, or if you're now making $40,000 a year and it's not likely that you'll ever make much more in your current job, you're headed for a long spell of unhappiness. In fact, you may not ever feel happy.

Does this mean you shouldn't rank happiness as your most important value, or as a value at all? Possibly, but probably not. You have every right to be happy. However, be practical. If happiness is important to you, make some rules that will allow you to be happy *while you're en route to realizing* your long-term dreams, or targets.

Many people, by the way, have said upon accomplishing a dream that the real fun was in chasing it! Once they accomplished the dream, the fun was over. In other words, real happiness could be realized en route to the dream.

John Dewey said happiness "comes from the full participation of all our powers in the endeavor to wrest from each changing situation or experience its own full and unique meaning." Storm Jameson said, "Happiness comes of the capacity to feel deeply, to enjoy simply, to think freely, to risk life, to be needed."

Happiness may be easier to attain than you realize!

How can you achieve happiness while you're working on earning $150,000 a year, saving to buy a Rolls Royce and a vacation home in the Cayman Islands, and figuring out how you can do it all while only working two days a week? You can do it by appreciating some of the simpler joys of life.

Remember what Barbra Streisand said? "People who need people are the luckiest people in the world." I suppose she'd accept "happiest" as a substitute for "luckiest," just to help me make my point.

William Lyon Phelps said, "The happiest people are those who think the most interesting thoughts. Interesting thoughts can only live in cultivated minds. Those who decide to use leisure as a means of mental development, who love good music, good books, good pictures, good plays at the theater, good company, good conversation—what are they? They are the happiest people in the world; and they are not only happy in themselves, they are the cause of happiness in others."

Set yourself up to be happy about some short-term targets while you're striving to reach your long-term targets. For example, you could decide, "I'll derive satisfaction from every activity, including my job." You could also decide, "I'll be happy with every new opportunity." Or, "I'll be content to imagine what my life will be like when I finally accomplish my big dreams." And so on.

These rules then become your way of life. You must practice them daily. Violate them and you invalidate your value system—and you set yourself up to fail.

If you can't prescribe rules that will provide daily satisfaction, then maybe you should reevaluate your values. Perhaps you're not being realistic. If you can't possibly find happiness until you accomplish your long-term targets, your alternative may be misery! More than likely, however, you weren't realistic about establishing rules for yourself.

Here are some other examples of value-based rules.

For family: Spending one day every week together.

For security: Putting aside 10 percent of every paycheck and investing in low-risk savings plans.

For health: Avoiding caffeine and fatty foods, exercising daily, and getting an annual check-up.

For adventure: Enrolling in an Outward Bound course, or planning an exotic vacation.

It's important to note that your values can change, as can the conditions for fulfillment of your values. So it's necessary to monitor your value system periodically.

So the next step is to create rules that will allow you to receive immediate gratification as you fulfill each of your values. Under each of your values, list the rules you will observe. Do it now.

Rules for value #1

1. _____

2. _____

3. _____

4. _____

5. _____

Rules for value #2

1. _____

2. _____

3. _____

4. _____

5. _____

Rules for value #3

1. _____

2. _____

3. _____

4. _____

5. _____

Rules for value #4

1 _____

2. _____

3. _____

4. __ _____

5. _____

Rules for value #5

1. _____

2. _____

3. _____

4. _____

5. _____

Of course, as values and conditions change, so should

the rules that you prescribe for yourself.

If you acknowledge your value system, and you've established rules to live by, it's a lot easier to know what to do when faced with a decision.

Discover who you are and who you can be

I urge you to take the time to think about your values, develop a list of prioritized values if you haven't already done so, and prescribe the rules that will help you verify your value system. This is a powerful self-management tool. Not only does it provide a personal rule book for how to live your life, it also makes it easier for you to make important decisions. If you acknowledge your value system, and you've established rules to live by, it's a lot easier to know what to do when faced with a decision.

Not long ago I read a newspaper report about a couple who obviously knew their values and had prioritized them. One day Cheree Garrett asked her father why he and her mother weren't going off on trips and doing other activities in their retirement. And he told his daughter, "We're doing everything exactly the way we want." Not long thereafter, he died.

Cheree went home and asked her husband Jay, "Are we doing everything exactly the way we want?"

They weren't.

Jay had just celebrated his twentieth anniversary of working for the same utility company. Cheree managed a dental office. Unsatisfied with their lives, but unsure of what they wanted to do, the Garretts liquidated, bought a tent trailer, and headed south from Seattle. They finally stopped in Tucson.

For a couple of years they lived off their savings. Jay worked in real estate and then started his own wallpapering business. Cheree went back to managing a dental office.

One day they realized that, while they had changed their environment, they hadn't really changed their lives. So they dropped out again and started baking cookies, which they sold at rodeos. Friends went into business with them, and they projected earnings of $25,000 their first year. Instead, each couple netted $25.

Broke and discouraged, the Garretts were baking cookies one day when another friend suggested they try selling sandwiches. "We didn't know how to make sandwiches," Cheree explained in a newspaper article. "But that night we decided, 'Let's do it.'"

They sold 7 sandwiches their first day in business. But that number eventually increased to 50 a day, then 250, and finally, several years later, 1,400 sandwiches a day and growing.

The Garretts are a good example of what can happen when people follow their dreams, and fulfill their needs.

The wheel of life

Here's another exercise that will help you clarify your value system and, at the same time, prioritize your needs in life.

The "Wheel of Life" on the next page has six spokes, each representing a major area of life: financial, physical, social, mental, ethical/spiritual, and family. Using a scale of zero (at the center of the circle) to one hundred (at the outside edge of the circle) you can evaluate your current position on the wheel in each of the stated areas.

To demonstrate how the Wheel of Life works, I've already completed the sample shown below. This particular wheel diagrams the life of a fictitious character, whom I'll call "Michael." He's a fellow with a lot of turmoil in his life, and he doesn't know why.

Look at the financial spoke. Michael is now earning

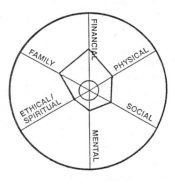

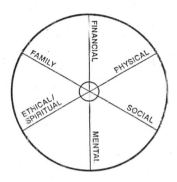

$20,000 a year, but he wants to earn $40,000. He's earning fifty percent of his target income, so I placed a slash mark at mid-point on the financial spoke.

Next, look at the physical spoke, which measures overall health. There's no point in becoming the richest person in town only to spend your money on hospital bills. So think about your health.

Michael's not in very good shape. He doesn't exercise at all, he needs to lose a little weight, and it's been several years since he visited the doctor for a physical exam. I gave him a 20 percent rating, and accordingly I placed a slash mark on the physical spoke not too far from the center of the wheel.

Socially, Michael tries hard. He has a wide circle of friends, but he doesn't spend enough time cultivating relationships. In addition, he doesn't relax, he never vacations, and he's feeling the stress of his job. He's about 20 percent on target. Michael has to learn how to "play." Once he does, he'll discover that it pays off both personally and on the job. I found out that some of my most creative ideas come to me when I'm on vacation, enjoying myself and the people around me.

The mental spoke measures continuing education. Unfortunately, too many people stop learning once they graduate from high school or college. We constantly need new information. And there are plenty of ways to get it. We can enroll in adult classes, attend seminars and workshops, read books, listen to tapes, and associate with stimulating people.

Poor Michael. He hasn't read a book since high school. He's never attended a seminar or workshop. But he does listen to tapes when he's driving in his car, and he reads some of his industry's trade publications. I scored him at 15 percent.

The ethical/spiritual spoke measures the way you treat people and the way you treat yourself, including how well you live up to your value system. It also measures your spiritual life.

Michael doesn't live up to his value system. He treats people ethically, fortunately, but he's got to improve his self-image if he's ever going to reach the success he desires. In addition, Michael is a church-goer, but that's the extent of his spirituality. He contributes neither time nor money to his church and does not exhibit other characteristics of a spiritual life. I scored him low, at 10 percent.

The final spoke on the Wheel of Life, family, measures your relationship with your family. Ultimately, family is probably our most important value. When everything else fades, family remains, if we've cultivated it.

Michael is learning to be a good family man. He spends individual time with each of his children, and he enjoys leisure time with his wife. The problem: he allows the stress of his job to interfere with his family life. Too often he disrupts the family because he's preoccupied with his work. In addition, he hardly ever spends time with his elderly parents. I scored him at 40 percent.

After evaluating each area of life, connect the slash marks. If there's balance in your life, the slash marks should form a circle. Take a look at Michael's "circle." It's grossly uneven, signifying that he doesn't have his priorities in order. No wonder he's in turmoil. (Of course, if Michael had scored 5 percent in each area, making a perfect circle, that would have been cause for concern as well!)

However, one look at the Wheel of Life and Michael can quickly determine where he needs to make improvements. Once he does, his overall life will be better.

Your business needs values & rules, too

To a great degree your business will reflect your personal

values, at least in the start-up years. This is why it's a good idea to identify your values before you go into business. After that, I suggest you form a set of rules for your business. Not only should you practice the rules, you should teach them to your employees and business associates as well.

I've always had a strong commitment to customer service and satisfaction in business. I learned this trait from the Safferin brothers, who owned a little pharmacy in Middle Village, New York, where I worked as a youngster.

The Safferins always displayed their merchandise in a pleasing way, but the goods on the shelf were merely props to the Safferins, who demonstrated customer service with a dramatic flair. They knew all of their customers by name, gave them advice, cheerfully responded to their idiosyncrasies, and made sure that each one of them left the store in a better frame of mind than when he entered. Some days the Safferins sent me ten miles down the road on my bicycle to deliver a small bottle of medicine to a customer who couldn't get to the store. The brothers realized they weren't the only pharmacists in town, and they taught me the importance of going out of my way for a customer.

By the time I started my own franchise company, Rainbow International, I had formed a set of values for myself, my employees, and franchisees. I listed the values on a large sign which now hangs in the lobby of my main office building, where everyone who enters can immediately see them. These values now serve all of my business enterprises, and I'm sharing them with you as an example of the values you might consider adapting for your own business.

Ten commandments of business success

1. We believe in superior service to our customers, our community, and to each other as members of the business community.
2. We believe that if we count our blessings every day, we keep the "negatives" away.
3. We believe that success is the result of clear, cooperative, positive thinking.

4. We believe that to build our business we must re-earn our positions every day by excelling in every way.

5. We believe that management should seek out what people are doing right and treat every associate in a friendly, fair, frank and firm way.

6. We believe that problems should be welcomed tranquilly and used as learning experiences.

7. We believe our Creator put us on earth to win. We will keep faith with His wishes by winning honestly and accepting our daily successes humbly, knowing that a higher power has guided us to victory.

8. We believe in the untapped potential of every human being. Every person we help achieve that potential will bring us one step closer to achieving our potential.

9. We believe that loyalty adds consistency to our lives.

10. We believe in building our country through the free enterprise system. We will demonstrate this belief by constantly attracting people to seek opportunity.

These are the values that nurture success in my businesses and in my personal life. Similar values, personally and professionally, will nurture success in your life and business, too.

ACTION ITEM

An early victory is always a great way to boost your self-confidence and motivate you to continue making progress toward a target. What kind of target doesn't matter.

Athletic events, sales competitions, learning something new—if you get an early victory in the process, the rest of the battle is just a bit

continued on next page

easier. So what I'd like you to do now is consult the list of rules you created earlier in this chapter. Select any one of the rules that you can accomplish *today*. It doesn't matter what it is. Just make sure it's something you can do today, and preferably in a short period of time. For example, if you said one of your rules would be to help one person daily, you could complete that target rule today. Do it! And experience the joy and the satisfaction of completing just one rule. That one victory will lead you to many more.

8.
Hidden Talents, New Opportunities

"By resources, I'm not just talking about the amount of money you've got in the bank. No, resources are much broader than dollars and cents."

"Investigate some opportunities!"

DON DWYER

Remember when you were a kid and you could be anything you wanted to be? There were no boundaries in childhood. Remember? One day a little boy was going to grow up to be a fireman, and the next day he changed his mind, deciding instead that he'd like to be a professional wrestler like Hulk Hogan. A little girl was going to become a lawyer, or a president, or a doctor, maybe even own a business. Anything was possible in childhood.

And why not? This is, after all, America, where the "If-he-can,-why-not-me?" perspective of youth actually makes a lot of sense.

"The great man is he who does not lose his child's heart," said Menicus.

Unfortunately, our possibilities narrowed with age. By the time we were young adults, we defined our futures in terms of our education, our money, our jobs, and what people (parents, teachers, relatives, etc.) told us we could become. What happened is that we closed ourselves into a box, and with each passing year of age, the box got smaller and smaller. One day, we woke up, and the box was tiny.

You can always tell when someone is accepting the limits of his or her tiny box. That person says "no" to all sorts of opportunities.

You can always tell when someone is accepting the limits of his or her tiny box. That person says "no" to all sorts of opportunities. He or she uses phrases like these:

- I can't sell.
- I can't afford it.
- Maybe after the kids have gotten older . . .
- I don't know how.
- I haven't got the knack for that.
- I don't have enough education.
- I'm too old . . . too young . . . too . . .
- I don't know the right people.
- I don't have the money.
- I can't get the money.
- I don't have the time.

Most people who live in tiny boxes never even investigate their options and opportunities. And the sad fact is that these people are frequently young, perhaps twenty-five or thirty.

Of course, the people who live in these tiny boxes are constantly scratching to get out. If only they knew how. They wish for a nicer home, a better car, a different job or business, a bigger bank account. They wish they could trade places with this neighbor or that relative. But they quickly suppress these disturbing, painful thoughts. They believe, after all, that the "haves" possess some mystical, magical combination of talents that were denied to everyone else. As a result, most people who live in tiny boxes never even *investigate* their options and opportunities. And the sad fact is that these people are frequently young, perhaps twenty-five or thirty.

Lewis Dunnington wrote, "What life means to us is determined not so much by what life brings to us as by the attitude we bring to life; not so much by what happens to us as by our reaction to what happens."

Fortunately for me, I never closed myself into a tiny box. My insatiable curiosity, and my insistent belief that anyone could do anything, including me, continues to lead me to investigate options and opportunities every day of my life. By so doing, I've been able to discover what I'm good at, and also what makes me happy. Most people simply never make these great discoveries because they refuse to investigate.

By investigating options and opportunities, I worked in a retail store and a factory, I sold real estate, I attended college, I built a newspaper route business with a team of delivery people, I ran a restaurant and a night club, managed entertainers, produced records, worked as an executive in a corporation, sold and marketed franchises, bought real estate, built a new, multi-faceted franchise organization, and recruited people who wanted to become successful business owners.

Now you might look at that list and find few similarities linking one job to another, but each job prepared me for the next one. And each represented an intense investigation of what that job was all about.

What are you investigating now?
If you're one of those people who's trapped inside a tiny box, investigation will set you free. So far, you've bought the box. You decided not to investigate. And if you continue living in that box, you can predict what your life will be like next year, five years from now, even ten years from now. It won't be all that different from the way it is right now.

There are tens of thousands of ways to earn a living in America. People make excellent incomes in big cities and small towns. Just open your eyes and your mind as you drive slowly through the streets of your town. You'll pass by shopping centers, office buildings, businesses of all sorts, and you'll see the wide variety of job opportunities displayed. Not that you want a job. I assume you want to own a business. But just take a look at all the different kinds of businesses that provide jobs.

You don't want to drive through town? Fine. Open your telephone directory to the Yellow Pages and take a look at all the businesses. Or pick up the newspaper and look at the Help Wanted and Business Opportunities sections. Or visit your library and browse through the business section.

Investigate some opportunities!

One who broke out

While I was writing this chapter, I received a letter from one of our franchise owners in Las Vegas who is a perfect example of how people break out of those tiny boxes. Actually, the letter was addressed to one of my executive vice presidents, the man who runs our franchise company, Worldwide Refinishing. But let me share the story with you. It will show you how a thirty-year-old, "down-and-out" waitress traded in her daily routine for a career of "fun, joy, and wealth."

Barbara Turns was the mother of two young daughters and married to a man who was apparently not happy. They lived in Las Vegas. She was a waitress and he was a painter. One day a friend called Barbara and told her about a bathtub refinishing business that the friend thought might be a good opportunity for Barbara's husband. But when Barbara told her husband about it, he laughed.

"Why would anyone want to buy a refinished bathtub for $250," he said, "when you can buy a new tub for $80?" Then he told Barbara, "If you think it's such a good opportunity, you do it." However, he said he would have nothing to do with such a business.

At first, Barbara was defeated, knocked back down into her tiny box. "I always felt that to be successful you had to be lucky, or born into wealth," she writes. But when she heard that a woman in Texas owned one of the franchises, and was successful, "Then my interest [was] piqued. I don't know why, I just knew that if I was to survive I would have to create my future, and this seemed as good a plan as any for keeping us off welfare."

In February 1990, having secured a second mortgage

on her home, and in spite of everyone's telling her that she was about to make a dreadful mistake, Barbara invested in a franchise. During her first training session, she recalls, "My heart sank. My husband was right. I was a girl. What made me think I could refinish a bathtub?" Even though she struggled through the training program, and passed, she went home discouraged.

Worse news awaited her in Las Vegas. Her husband had quit his job and moved to California. "I had no idea when he was coming back, or even if he was coming back, so I did what any desperate female would do. I cried, and then I cried some more, and some more."

But then, "It hit me. Las Vegas was booming. There were a million bathtubs out there being chipped by the dozens." Barbara began visiting construction sites, handing out her business card to the superintendents. And soon, "My bathtub repair business was off and running."

That first year, Barbara grossed $35,000 in about ten months. The second year, 1991, she grossed $94,000. Her husband, by the way, never returned. Barbara was divorced and has since remarried. Her present husband works with her in the business, and at the time of writing this letter, she said, "We just signed two contracts with two major hotels in Las Vegas to refinish more than three hundred tubs. . . . Where will I go from here? Only the Lord knows. I have learned to follow my dreams. To take each day and shoot for one goal at a time. And I am going for it!"

It is unusual for a woman, and a former waitress, to become the owner of a service business that repairs and refinishes bathtubs and other fixtures, but these things can happen! In our organization, people come to us from many different occupations. Some of our franchise owners were formerly coaches, teachers, social workers, sales executives, hair stylists, clerks, bus drivers, housewives.

What made them different? Like Barbara, they got out of their boxes. They investigated their options and opportunities. They stopped saying, "I don't . . . I can't . . . I won't . . . I lack . . ." and they knocked down the walls of their tiny boxes.

To quote Barbara, "Searching for, finding, and achieving what makes you happy in life is the secret to success.

And that takes honesty, hard work, and soul searching." I would add, it takes investigation, too.

How to be a good investigator

If one of your dreams is to get into business for yourself, you've got to do some investigating of the options and opportunities that exist. Here are four steps to follow:

1. The broad overview

Get out and discover what's going on in the world!

If you're like most people, you follow the same routine day in and day out. You get up in the morning and you either eat breakfast or don't. If you do, you eat the same foods for breakfast almost daily. Maybe you read the morning newspaper, or watch the morning news. Whatever it is, you have your routine.

Then you drive to work. Maybe you walk, or maybe you ride a bike, or a bus. But however you go to work, you get there the same way every day. You see the same people, the same sights. You probably even say the same words over and over, every morning, to the same people.

At work, you also have a routine. If you're a coffee drinker, that's your first assignment: to get a cup of coffee. Then you get to work. Whatever it is you do, you probably do it the same way every day, eight hours a day. Until it's time to go home.

And how do you go home? The same way you got to work. You just backtrack. Now you see the same people again. The same sites. You say the same words, only now you say, "Have a good evening," instead of "Have a good day."

And at home, what do you do? Most Americans watch television. If you do, I bet you watch the same programs week after week. At some point you eat dinner. Nothing unusual about it, either. If it's Monday, it's fish. If it's Tuesday, it's chicken. And so on. You got the idea. Life, for most people, becomes a routine, surrounded by four walls of a tiny box. People who live like this are "out of it," as the kids say. I hope you're "into it."

I hope you're into living. Into investigating options and opportunities. Into searching, finding and achieving.

If you're guilty of living a routine, change it. Start

small, then get bolder. When you drive to work, take a different route. Look around you. What's happening out there?

If you usually listen to the radio while you drive, change the station, or put a tape in the cassette player if you have one. Tune in to different ideas.

Drive to the newsstand and buy six magazines that you've never read before. Buy an out-of-town newspaper. Find out what people are reading, buying, selling.

Instead of turning on the television set at home, read. Ugh. I can hear the groans. "No one reads anymore." True. They just pull the walls of their tiny boxes around them even tighter.

But not you! Now that you've got the broad overview, you're getting "into it."

2. *Agree to change*

At the moment, you may have a "locked in" view of what you're good at, what you're not, and what you can and can't do. But I bet you haven't tested those concepts for years. Maybe it's time for a change?

When we're faced with change, it's a frightening thing. We resist it. We don't like to make ourselves vulnerable. We don't like to show our weaknesses. Of course, we can always choose to crawl back into that tiny box and suffocate!

To grow, we must change. And no matter how good we get at whatever it is we do, or how successful we become, there's always something to change.

The fact is, to grow, we must change. And no matter how good we get at whatever it is we do, or how successful we become, there's always something to change.

Tony Robbins, who's become famous in recent years on the motivational lecture circuit, is responsible for one of the most profound changes that occurred in my life. We were driving from Dallas to Waco one day, talking about the future growth of my organization, when Tony asked me a question:

"Why don't you open up and let people know you care about them?"

Wow! I thought I did. But as we talked about it, I realized that while I had made some improvements in this area of my life, I still had a long way to go.

Immediately I began to explore the options and opportunities. I attended some seminars. I read more. I tried to understand what was holding me back. The environment that I had grown up in made me a cautious person. Emotionally, I protected myself.

So I adapted techniques that would force me to become more open. For example, I spoke to people first, rather than waiting for them to speak to me. I'd get on an elevator and say hello to the people inside. I saw the benefits at once. People want to be recognized, even by a stranger. The wonderful thing about the human race is that basically we're all the same, worldwide. We've all got the same emotional needs.

Gradually, I was able to feel comfortable telling people I cared. Know what? Not only have I benefited personally from letting people know that I care about them, my organization has prospered, too. I've been able to attract top talent because people want to work for me rather than someone else.

I made the decision to change. And I did.

When you decide to make changes, you'll make a difference in your life. You have hidden talents and abilities. Maybe there's a tiny box smothering them.

3. Explore business opportunities

I don't know what kind of business would be right for you, but I believe there's a business for everyone who wants one. You've got to take a look at what's available.

Go to the newsstand, the bookstore, or the library and you'll find a dozen different magazines and at least a few books that list business opportunities, including franchises. Your Sunday newspaper may list business opportunities and franchises for sale. Depending on where you live, you might discover a nearby business expo or a franchise fair at which you'll have the opportunity to see numerous businesses on display during one weekend. If one of these events isn't happening in your town, they're happening almost every weekend in major cities across the USA. Drive to one of them.

Explore business opportunities by gathering as much literature as you possibly can, and then talk to people who operate similar businesses. Build files about the businesses that interest you the most and pay attention to what the owners of these businesses have to say. What you're trying to do is figure out whether you'd like to own and operate the same kind of business.

Chances are you won't find a business that you can say you love everything about it. I'll admit that there are some things about my business that I don't like! For example, I hate meeting with the numbers crunchers, the accountants. Ugh! I'm not interested in hours of discussing tax matters, payroll issues, ratios, and balance sheets. Not my idea of fun. I also don't like to deal with insurance matters, logistical details, or firing people.

Each of our franchisees will tell you there are things about their businesses that they don't like. I can't imagine, for example, any one of them having a passionate love for cleaning carpets, unclogging drains, or refinishing bathtubs!

Even so, our franchisees love their businesses for the same reason I love mine: it's rewarding. We like being useful to other people. We like productive work and happy customers. We like managing a team of people. We like the identity that our businesses give us in our communities. We enjoy our good business reputations. We like being regarded as successful, hard-working people.

You can find a business opportunity that will grant you similar results. To make sure you do, take the time to evaluate each of the activities and responsibilities involved in any business that interests you. We have a rule at The Dwyer Group that before we'll allow prospective investors to acquire one of our franchises, they must first work for a day or two, longer if they'd like, with one of our franchisees. That way, they get the experience of owning and operating the business without making a financial commitment. I think it's a great idea.

You want to own a restaurant business? Fine. Go to work at a restaurant, preferably the kind you'd like to own. You want to own a bookstore? Great. Go to work in a bookstore. You want to own a retail shop? There are plenty of opportunities. But work in a similar retail shop before you make the decision to commit your money and talents.

Also, by working in different businesses, even part-time, you'll learn a little something here, a little something there, and you'll eventually carry all of that wisdom into the business you decide to own. Lessons that I learned in my newspaper business, my restaurant business, and my talent management business are still helping me today.

At the end of this chapter you'll find two exercises to help you work through these issues.

4. Marshal your resources

The fourth investigative step is to get a grasp on your resources . . . even the ones you don't know you own!

Don't slide backward now. It would be easy to crawl back into that tiny box and say, "But I don't have any resources." Don't do it. You've come a long way already!

By resources I'm not just talking about the amount of money you've got in the bank. No, resources are much broader than dollars and cents.

Resources include the people you know. Not to borrow money from them, necessarily, but to pick their brains. I suggest you make a list of people you know who are successful in business. Relatives, friends, neighbors, former teachers, anyone at all. Now, make a point to call them, talk to them. Tell them what you'd like to do. Can they help? What can they suggest? Whom do they know who might give you some advice? And yes, if you think you're going to need financial help, don't be afraid to say so. There could be someone willing to back you, or invest with you, or loan you the money. I see it happen almost every day.

Resources include your continuing education. Whether or not you've got a college education isn't important. Remember, your past does not determine your future. That's not to say, however, that you shouldn't enroll in a course at a local college. Courses such as *Starting Your Own Business* and *How To Buy A Franchise* are frequently taught at colleges or are available through business associations. Find out if there's a similar course being offered in your area. If you have to, drive a distance to get to one!

Resources include money. And usually, people who want to start a business don't have enough money—they think.

Every day our franchise counselors work with people who want to invest in a franchise opportunity but say they can't afford the investment. Frequently they can. In chapter 11 I'll discuss how to acquire start-up and operating capital.

For now, let me suggest that you not allow a lack of financial resources to stop you from acquiring your own business. That would be the same as crawling back into your tiny box!

These four steps just outlined are time-consuming. But the payoff can be tremendous.

Business self-evaluation
Most of your waking hours are spent earning a living. So now I suggest you take an inventory of your talents and abilities. This exercise will help you evaluate your career targets. If you don't know the answer to any of the following questions, just say to yourself: "I don't know the answer, but if I did know, what would I say?"

1. What do I enjoy doing in my work life?

A. _____

B. _____

C. _____

D. _____

E. _____

2. What don't I enjoy doing in my work life?

A. _____

B. _____

C. _____

D. _____

E. _____

3. What are my strengths?

A. _____

B. _____

C. _____

D. _____

E. _____

4. What are my weaknesses?

A. _____

B. _____

C. _____

D. _____

E. _____

5. To be successful in business, what changes will I have to make?

A. _____

B. _____

C. _____

D. _____

E. _____

6. Why would I have to make those changes?

A. _____

B. _____

C. _____

D. _____

E. _____

7. Am I willing to take the steps necessary to make these changes?

_____

_____

8. Why am I willing to make these changes now?

_____

_____

9. Five years from now, having made these changes, what will my life be like?

_____

_____

10. Will the rewards be greater than the efforts I will have to expend to make these changes in my life?

_____

_____

Business dream list
The purpose of this exercise is to help you expand your mind to the business opportunities that await you. Make a list of the businesses that appeal to you. Make the list as long or as short as you like. After you make the list, prioritize the businesses. The first prioritized business would be the one that you'd most like to own. Then, divide the list into two A&B lists. In the A list, include the five businesses you'd most like to own. In the B list, include the five businesses that you can afford, and would most like to own.

Dream list of businesses I like (in priority order)

1. _____

2. _____

3. _____

4. _____

5. _____

6. _____

7. _____

8. _____

9. _____

10. _____

11. _____

12. _____

Top five businesses I'd most like to own

1. _____

2. _____

3. _____

4. _____

5. _____

Top five businesses I'd most like to own, and can afford

1. _____

2. _____

3. _____

4. _____

5. _____

Finding your dream business

   The purpose of this exercise is to help you analyze the businesses you'd most like to own. I encourage you to ask questions about these businesses to make certain that they're consistent with your targets and values. The exercise will help you make a better decision when you finally do invest in a business.

1. Is there a market for the product or service this business offers?

_____

_____

2. Will the product or service have public appeal for many years to come?

_____

_____

3. Can this business grow to meet my ultimate income targets?

_____

_____

4. Will the business grow in value so that I will be able to sell the business for a price equal to the money and effort I have invested?

_____

_____

5. Will the area where I locate this business have a need for the product/service I offer in five, ten, twenty, or thirty years?

_____

_____

6. Will I have an opportunity to grow as a person in the company or industry?

_____

_____

7. Do I like the people I will associate with in this company or industry?

_____

_____

8. Will being part of this company or industry add value to my family life?

_____

_____

9. How competitive is the business in my city or town?

_____

_____

10. How will I handle the competition?

_____

_____

11. Have I personally talked to the competitors?

_____

_____

12. Will I personally talk to and visit with the people who now do business with the company I plan to buy or join? While I am visiting them, will I get answers to the questions I ask?

_____

_____

13. Have I sought professional counsel in reviewing the financial and legal aspects of my decision to invest in this business? (Caution: Ask your accountant for accounting advice and your attorney for legal advice. But you make the business decisions! People who practice these two professions have killed more good deals than they have made).

_____

_____

14. Am I emotionally committed to do what it takes to grow the business?

_____

_____

15. Is my spouse supportive of my decision to own my own business?

_____

_____

16. Does my spouse know as much as I do about the business?

_____

_____

17. Have I completed a one-year business plan?

_____

_____

18. Do I have a two-to-three-month reserve of credit or capital if needed in the initial stages of launching the business?

_____

_____

19. Will I be happy owning and operating this business?

_____

_____

ACTION ITEM

I doubt that anyone grows personally and financially without changing _something_. It's painful to change, but it's necessary. Today I want you to identify a change that you need to make in your life. It doesn't have to be a major change. And it may not be possible for you to complete the change today. But whatever you decide to change, think of something that you can do immediately to begin the process. And then do it now!

9.
Getting Off to the Right Start

"The annual failure rate in franchising is significantly less than among independent business start-ups, where it's at least one-third, if not half. I like that edge."

"Today, I am still convinced that franchise ownership is the best way for the first-time entrepreneur to get started in business."

DON DWYER

The first few times I was invited to advise people about investing in a business, I was faced with two interesting questions.

For many years I've been helping people get started in new business ventures through franchising, and only through franchises of The Dwyer Group. As the owner of a franchise conglomerate, I assume people would expect me to preach the franchise story, because franchise ownership is what I sell.

When I first went into business, I selected a franchise, not just once, but twice. My newspaper route was actually a franchise. It was loosely organized, and no one back then thought of it as a franchise, but I had a prescribed territory and a system to follow.

My second business—the dealership that I purchased from Success Motivation Institute—was also a franchise. It was much better organized than the newspaper route business, but it operated in a similar fashion.

Back when I was getting my business career underway, I believed that franchising was the best way to structure a win-win business relationship, and the most practical way to rapidly build a large organization of successful business people.

But neither my bias about franchising, nor my personal sales interests, were reasons for inviting me to give people my advice on television, or via an audiocassette program, or in the pages of a magazine or book. No, I was expected to lay out the facts and allow the chips to fall where they belonged. Anyone who listened to my advice would then be free to make his or her own decisions about business ownership.

I couldn't agree more. So whenever I was asked to speak under those circumstances, I first revisited my ideas about franchising. Would I still advise people to invest in a franchise opportunity, as opposed to going into business independently? And if there were no chance that someone was going to buy one of my franchises, would I still advise that person to consider buying another franchise opportunity?

After a long period of reflecting on these questions, I ended up where I had started. My answer to both questions was a resounding Yes! Today I am still convinced that franchise ownership is the best way for the first-time entrepreneur to get started in business.

Find a network and join it

Thinking back over the hundreds of franchisees I've known, I can assure you that many of them, maybe most of them, wouldn't have succeeded in business without the support of a franchise network. It didn't have to be my franchise network, so long as it was a good franchise network.

Sal Aiello is a franchisee who comes to mind. He was a grocery store clerk in Chico, California, when I met him. Sal had grown up in a family of hard-working commercial fishermen. Sal's people made a living, but Sal wanted something more than an average income. And he was willing to follow my advice to succeed in business.

In fact, even before Sal became one of my franchisees, he started following my system for success. He needed money to buy a franchise, and he didn't have it. We told him how to get it, step by step, and he did. Sal now owns a business that grosses more than $300,000 a year. He has hit every target that he's set, including the acquisition of a four-thousand-square-foot home on a six-acre ranch. Not long ago I heard from Sal, and he said, "There's no doubt that your system and support is a major factor in our continuing success."

Of course, all of this may sound self-serving to you, because, let's face it, I do own and sell franchises. But I hope you won't allow that to get in the way of hearing my message. Should you buy one of my franchises and join our international network? Maybe. But let me tell you, my organization is just one of a few hundred, if not more than a thousand, that's booming. Across this country, and in other countries, there are many well-managed, high-quality franchise networks that offer you the opportunity to succeed in business, and in life. If one of my franchise opportunities doesn't interest you, one of the others surely will. And that's what's important to me in this book.

Now, strike oil!
Asked for his advice, J. Paul Getty said, "Rise early. Work late. Strike oil." And there certainly are entrepreneurs, year after year, who "strike oil" in various ways. They invent a new technology, like Steven Jobs, who started Apple Computers. Or they have remarkable vision, extraordinary timing, and awesome persistence—like Ray Kroc, who knew exactly what to do when he stumbled across the McDonald brothers' little drive-in.

But most successful business people, and in fact, most people who become millionaires, do not follow in the exotic, exciting, headline-making model suggested by J. Paul Getty. Most become successful and make their money quietly, in ordinary businesses managed expertly and effectively. Most begin as working people, with little to invest but their time. They are the first-time entrepreneurs, and they help themselves immensely when they join a solid franchise network that indeed can help them strike oil!

Consider the franchise option

What makes me so sure that franchising is the way to go?

Security. Calculated risk. You'll recall from an earlier chapter that one of the characteristics of a successful entrepreneur is to calculate every move. Investing in a franchise—with some exceptions—should never be a risky gamble.

Franchisees benefit from a relationship with a parent company, commonly called the franchisor. The strength of the parent company, assuming that it's operated responsibly, is drawn from its network of franchisees and then fed back to its franchisees. The franchisor not only creates a system for operating the franchise business but teaches the system to its franchisees, and continues to improve the system based on the experiences of its franchisees. It's an evolutionary relationship that should continue growing stronger year after year. And as it does, both franchisor and franchisees should become more successful.

While franchising has existed in the United States since at least the late 1800s, it's only become popular in the post-World War II era. When people hear the word "franchising," they frequently think first of McDonald's, indeed one of the finest franchise networks in the world. Then they may think of other fast-food enterprises, some of which also have become business legends.

But most people are surprised to hear that there are more than three thousand different franchise opportunities offered in the United States. Sixty different industries use franchising as a means of business expansion. Fast food is only one of those industries. You name the industry today and there's probably a franchise network within that industry. If not, it's likely there will be one day soon.

You might be surprised to know that a new franchise opens in America every sixteen minutes! Imagine that. Almost four times an hour. There are twenty million businesses in America and more than a quarter of them are franchise outlets. And the number is rapidly expanding.

Every new franchise creates, on average, eight new jobs. While Fortune 500 companies lost more than three million jobs in the 1980s, franchise businesses created 1.8 million new jobs.

Surprising, too, is the number of jobs created by franchises. In 1991, more than seven million people worked in franchise businesses. Every new franchise creates, on average, eight new jobs. While Fortune 500 companies lost more than three million jobs in the 1980s, franchise businesses created 1.8 million new jobs.

Now do you understand why I'm sold on franchising?

Let me give you one more reason, tracking back to the issue of security. No one knows for sure how many franchise businesses fail each year. Government statistics have reported a failure rate under five percent. Some independent studies have reported higher failure rates. Indeed, some franchise systems have failed altogether. But overall, the annual failure rate in franchising is significantly less than among independent business start-ups, where it's at least one-third, if not half. I like that edge. And when you become a franchise owner, you automatically benefit from this track record.

Two kinds of franchises

There are basically two kinds of franchises: business format and trademark licensing.

1. The business-format franchise.

Regardless of your experience with franchises, you're most familiar with business format franchises. These are the 7-Elevens, the Holiday Inns, the Jiffy Lubes, and also hundreds of home-based service businesses that don't operate from storefronts. These are all system-oriented businesses.

The franchisor sells to the franchisees a proven system for success, taking into account the ABCs of business operations. Training, product support, advertising and marketing services, and a home-office staff to provide continuing guidance are all part of the package. And (this is also true of trademark licenses) business-format franchises frequently provide instant recognition in the marketplace. McDonald's golden arches, for example, look the same in Honolulu as they do in Kansas City, New York City, and even Moscow.

A business-format franchise gives every entrepreneur a track to run on, and that's particularly important to the

---

Success in a business format franchise is not dependent on trial and error, or good luck. The risks have been minimized. Others have proven that the program works.

---

first-time entrepreneur. Success in a business-format franchise is not dependent on trial and error, or good luck. The risks have been minimized. Others have proven that the program works. If the franchisee is willing to accept the leadership of the franchisor and to follow directions, the battle for business success is half won.

The job of the business-format franchisor is counseling, assisting franchisees with all of their business challenges, leading, motivating, and persuading. As Ray Kroc said, business-format franchising is a way for you to "be in business for yourself, but not by yourself."

By the way, many business-format franchises are service businesses, and I especially want to draw your attention to this category. There's been an incredible boom in service industries, and that's where you may find your best opportunities.

We live in an age when everyone is "time poor." Husbands and wives both work, sometimes for choice, sometimes for economic reasons, sometimes both. But as a result, no one has any free time to do the things our parents used to handle without much difficulty.

Consequently, people are willing to pay for many services today. Carpet cleaning, bathtub refinishing, drain maintenance, maid services, gardening, catering, construction, home decorating, financial services—and the list goes on and on.

Starting and expanding a service business usually requires less money, and is easier to operate, than most retail businesses, restaurants, or manufacturing businesses. I encourage you to take a close look at the opportunities among service franchise businesses, especially if they are of the business format variety.

2. Trademark licensing.

You're familiar with many of these franchises, too. Coca-Cola, Chevrolet, professional sports teams, certain tire manufacturers, appliance manufacturers, and so on. In these franchise relationships, the franchisee is granted the right to market a particular product, but that's the end of the story. Trademark licensors do not provide a system for success. They are product-oriented, and for that reason, not recommended for first-time entrepreneurs. There's nothing wrong with these businesses. In fact, people compete to buy them. But they are for savvy entrepreneurs.

Evaluating franchise opportunities

Ultimately, you will make the decision about whether franchising is the way for you to get into business. If you decide that it is, then here are several points you should consider.

1. Evaluate the system

The heart and soul of every successful business, franchise or not, is the system. The system makes the business "foolproof." It removes the necessity of reinventing the wheel, or trial and error. A system allows you to concentrate on growing the business, achieving your targets, and fulfilling your business and personal needs.

The system is critically important to your investment. Make sure it exists, and make certain that it works. How can you tell whether it works? Talk to existing franchisees who use the system. They'll tell you!

Let me give you two examples of how the system works at Rainbow International.

In our businesses, the system accounts for every move that a franchisee makes during the course of a day. For example, Rainbow International franchisees are taught exactly how to ask for and get three referrals from each client whose carpet they clean or dye. By following this single instruction, franchisees generate about sixty referrals a week. That's three thousand referrals a year! Of that number, based on our collective experience, about six hundred referrals will become new clients. If the average job is worth $100, this single instruction guarantees our franchisees an extra $60,000 a year! Now, the person who goes into the same business without the benefit of our system may leave behind $30,000, $60,000, even $90,000 a year, simply because they have yet to figure out how the business works.

The second example: To expand a business, you have to multiply it. Rainbow International franchisees multiply by adding trucks. Each new truck or van that a franchisee puts on the road will generate an additional $15,000 net income. In addition, our franchisees have the opportunity to invest in two complementary businesses: Worldwide Refinishing and Mr. Rooter. By owning all three businesses, one franchisee can offer three different services to the same client base. This innovative multiplier provides higher sales for our franchisees while keeping their marketing costs minimal.

These are just two of the benefits of our franchise system. Other franchise systems are equally good. Your challenge is to go out and find them!

2. Expect full disclosure

One of the great advantages to buying a franchise is the disclosure law. Many franchisors will grumble about this cumbersome and costly law, which is mandated by the Federal government and even more stringently enforced in certain states. But it's good for franchising, and good for anyone who investigates a franchise offering.

In 1979, the Federal Trade Commission passed into law a Franchise Rule stating that franchisors must provide to prospective franchise investors a disclosure document, or Uniform Franchise Offering Circular. This document requires the franchisor to reveal detailed information about twenty-one aspects of the business, including names and addresses of existing and past franchisees, a financial statement, financial requirements of the franchisee, business background of the franchisor, and much more.

A good franchisor, in my opinion, will happily disclose all pertinent information about the business to prospective franchisees. Should you discover a franchisor who refuses to give you this information, or even hesitates, I would recommend that you continue looking at other opportunities.

By the way, it is illegal for a franchisor to accept your money, or ask you to sign a franchise agreement, without first giving you a copy of the disclosure document and allowing you to examine it for ten business days.

3. Buy brand-name identity

It's not always possible to buy a brand-name franchise, but it's an advantage when you can. Joining a business network that owns a share of its market gets you off to a fast start in business. Creating identity, and winning a share of the marketplace, may take years if you try to do it on your own.

Granted, every brand name had to begin somewhere. McDonald's, after all, is only forty years old. Domino's is younger. So is Subway, and Mailboxes Etc., and Decorating Den, and Sonic Industries, and Kwik Kopy, and many other major franchise brands. Then, too, some brand names are regional, not national. Sonic comes to mind. If you can afford to grow with a brand name, that's still a good investment.

By the way, not all franchises are start-up opportunities. Franchisees have been known to make their money, sell their businesses, and retire. Resales of franchises are plentiful, and these businesses have already established their names in the marketplace. Of course, a resale is usually more expensive than a start-up opportunity, because the original franchisee has already established the business.

4. Evaluate the training program

Good franchisors provide both a crash course to get a franchisee started in business and ongoing, follow-up training programs to help franchisees improve their business skills.

The crash course typically lasts for a week or two, usually at the franchisor's home office. In some cases a franchisor will spend a few days to a week in the franchisee's marketplace, helping to establish the business. Then the franchisor will organize regional meetings and an annual meeting, at which time there will be refresher courses and new training components. The training program should also include publications, audio and video tapes, and other supportive materials.

I believe a good training program goes beyond the technical aspects of building a business. I think it should also cover the psychological components, including many of the same issues we're discussing in this book. Frankly, many franchisors don't cover this information, and that's a big mistake. I believe we've done more for our franchisees by showing them how to overcome fears, how to dream, how to target, how to investigate new options and opportunities, than if we had merely taught them how to clean and dye carpets, or repair a bathtub, or clear a drain.

5. Look for purchasing power

One of the big financial advantages of joining a franchise network is purchasing power. Ideally, a franchisor arranges discounts for the franchisees. Products, supplies, equipment—even professional services, such as travel, and personal services, such as insurance—can be purchased at a discount by a franchise network.

The franchisor negotiates with suppliers and vendors on behalf of the franchisees and provides tremendous savings, which can be passed on to customers. These discounts can be significant, and they account for additional profits to the franchisees. Non-franchised businesses, or non-networked businesses, do not enjoy this purchasing power.

6. Evaluate the research & development

In today's fast-changing, very demanding marketplace, you can't survive in business without good R&D, meaning research and development. A business needs new products, new services. And yet, how does the independent business owner manage to staff and support an R&D department? It's costly. And it's nearly impossible to do.

Franchisees shouldn't have to worry about R&D. That's the franchisor's responsibility. The franchisor will maintain an ongoing R&D department, which will introduce new ideas for the franchise network to market and sell. Many of those good ideas, by the way, will come directly from the franchisees!

7. Look for expansion opportunities

If you invest in a franchise, it may be that you can only afford one territory or unit at first. Later you may want to add a second territory or unit. I think a good franchisor should help you with that expansion. A good franchisor should grant franchisees first crack at additional outlets, neighboring territories, or new franchises within the same organization.

8. Evaluate future value

Determining the future value of a franchise is not always easy to do. You've got to be a visionary—and frankly, you've got to guess right. Look at McDonald's. It's very difficult to buy one of those franchises today, particularly if you're a first-time entrepreneur. But back when Ray Kroc was selling franchises, he couldn't give away the units. Can you believe it was possible to buy a McDonald's for as little as $5,000? Those days are long gone.

But surely there are more companies like McDonald's on the horizon. And even some franchise businesses that don't become as popular as McDonald's will have high resale values. As a rule of thumb, franchises within a successful organization command a higher resale value than independent small businesses. Before you invest in a franchise, check out the resale price of franchises within the network. Also, make sure the franchisor will help you resell the franchise, but not limit the sales price.

Is franchising for everyone?

Some people should avoid franchising. In fact, there are two kinds of people who won't be happy in a franchise system.

The first is the fiercely independent entrepreneur. If you're that type, you bristle at direction and supervision, and you hate to conform to standards and policies. Complete independence may be a higher priority to you than profit, income, security, and overall success. In that case, a franchise system will produce stress in your business life rather than minimize it.

By the way, I appreciate the independent entrepreneur. I was one myself once. But I changed my value system once I experienced the synergy of a franchise network. Only you can decide what's more important to you.

The second kind of person who should avoid franchising is the one with a unique invention (a new product, or a new service) who thinks that franchising can make the invention popular. Franchising is a method of mass marketing, but it's for proven ideas, not new inventions. In these instances, I advise inventors to develop their own system before they try to franchise. Work out the bugs, make the product or idea marketable and salable, and prove that it can be profitable. Until then, stay clear of franchising.

When you consider the benefits of franchising, I think it's easy to understand why I've committed myself to that method of business and why I encourage others to do so as well.

ACTION ITEM

You can't really decide whether franchising is for you until you thoroughly investigate it and discover the thousands of different franchise opportunities that exist. Therefore, your Action Item today requires that you get a copy of at least one of the following publications, which can help you make decisions about investing in a franchise. The publications may be purchased at bookstores or newsstands, ordered directly from the publisher, or borrowed from your local library. I'm assigning you to get at least one of the publications, but all of them are valuable:

- *Franchise Opportunities Guide*, $20, published by the International Franchise Association, 1350 New York Ave., N.W., Washington, D.C. 20005, telephone: 202-628-8000. Available by mail and at many bookstores.
- *Investigate Before You Invest*, $5, published by the International Franchise Association. Available by mail.
- *Franchising: The Inside Story*, $18.95, published by TriMark. Telephone: 800-444-6670. Available by mail.
- The annual Entrepreneur Franchise 500, published by *Entrepreneur Magazine* every January. *Success Magazine*'s Top 100 and *Inc. Magazine*'s 500 Fastest Growing Companies are also important information sources. Available at newsstands.

10.
Six Laws of Multiplication

"You can recruit the world, but without self-esteem, people will lack the energy and drive to perform successfully."

"Praise is power!"

DON DWYER

You know that old saying about not being able to see the forest for the trees? That's what happens to many people who get into a business, any kind of business. They work so hard at it that they can never stop and visualize the whole picture. It's as if they're aiming at the bullseye, but the bullseye has become the entire target, rather than the center of a larger target.

Believe me, this is an easy trap to fall into. I've been there. It's like chasing your tail. You can make a good living doing that, if you can withstand the pressures, and the loneliness. But the problem is, you can't make any big money, because your income is limited by the size of your target.

If you're like most of the people I meet who want to get into business, you want to make the *big* money. Am I right?

That being the case, you'll want to know about my Six Laws of Multiplication.

1. People are power

You can't achieve great wealth by yourself. I didn't always believe that, by the way. I had to learn it, as I suspect most people do.

There was a time when I thought I could do everything better myself. No one could do things the way I could do them. This was the belief I held while I was building my newspaper distribution business. I had a terrific network of people working with me, but at that time I didn't think I had the patience to train other people. And even if I did, I didn't want to spend the time. So after I sold that business, I spent years searching for the perfect one-man business. I wanted unlimited growth potential. I wanted assured success. And I wanted very little human contact.

Well, I should have just bought a ticket for the lottery. Because I had a better chance of winning the lottery than discovering this fantasy business.

I went through the restaurant business, night clubs, managing talent, producing records—I even tried to duplicate the Woodstock festival. Hey, I always made good money. But I also always felt like a gerbil on a wheel, running round and round and round. No one could fault me for not working hard, but it would have been better had I learned the teamwork approach, which would have permitted me to work "smart" instead of "hard."

When I became a franchisee of Success Motivation Institute, I found out what I was doing wrong. Now picture this. SMI is a successful franchise business, even before Don Dwyer, but I was sure I knew more about the business than *they* did. They meaning the franchisor and the people at the home office.

So I decided I would become a senior vice president of the company. How was I going to do that? Very simple. I'd make myself the company's top salesperson by working round the clock seven days a week. I'd leave the house at dawn to get to a seminar or my first sales presentation, and I wouldn't get home until one or two a.m. I gave everything I had to the job, while my wife raised our family, practically alone. I was too busy being a one-man band to help. The sad thing was that I had given up the entertainment business for a franchise because talent management required a hectic travel schedule, keeping me away from home. But here I was, back in the trap.

I was progressing slowly at SMI. My job was to sell taped programs. I stored my inventory under the grand piano in our living room. One day I noticed that my stack of tapes wasn't getting any smaller. And suddenly the message hit me like a sledge hammer. That pile of tape albums was too big for me to *move* by myself, let alone sell! At that moment I realized my target was too small. I couldn't go any further than my own arms could stretch. I *had* to change my approach.

Well, the first thing I did was go on a recruitment campaign. I decided to hire people. I looked for entrepreneurs like me—hungry and ambitious people. In no time I had hired and trained more than a hundred new reps to work under my direction. My personal income almost instantly tripled, and by my first anniversary with the company, I was making more than $100,000 a year. That's when I was promoted to senior vice president.

And that's how I learned the all-important first rule of multiplication: People Are Power.

This rule is true in every business, but it's especially true in franchising, where you profit from the strengths of other people. The minute you buy a franchise, you get four advantages: (1) the knowledge and experience of the franchisor and others associated with the home office, including lawyers, marketers, real estate experts, and other professionals; (2) the franchise company's reputation (hopefully a good one); (3) purchasing power based on the network's volume; (4) the combined experience of your fellow franchisees, who can help you avoid costly mistakes and coach you through difficult problems.

2. Build self-esteem

The second law of multiplication is to build your own self-esteem and instill high self-esteem in others. Earlier in this book I talked about building your self-image, and the importance of doing so. It is, after all, the key to success.

But to enlarge your business target, and to break into the big money, you've got to build self-esteem in the people in your company. You can recruit the world, but without self-esteem people will lack the energy and drive to perform successfully.

The last thing a business owner needs is a staff of dependent people, warm bodies that don't make much happen. Where that condition exists, the business owner is usually guilty of failing to practice the second law of multiplication.

There's much you can do as a business owner to help people build self-esteem. We live in an age when motivational and personal growth books are published by the armloads. Bookstores devote entire sections to personal development tomes. Many of these books are issued as videotapes and audiotapes. Seminar companies make it possible for anyone to experience personal development adventures. All the business owner needs to do is tap into these opportunities. Start a company library. Pass around helpful books and tapes. Send your people to seminars, or bring the seminar to your company.

There's something else I recommend you do to build self-esteem among your people. Use my P.I.P. Theory (see P.I.P. Theory on page 123).

Part of the self-esteem building process is little victories. Help your people win little victories. I remember the first time a manager did this for me. I was working at SMI, and my mentor knew that I was afraid of public speaking. Studies have shown that huge numbers of people fear public speaking. In fact, I've heard people say they'd rather die than give a speech, and I think they meant it. I was surely afraid of it, although not enough to die.

But Jack Studnicky, my mentor at SMI, knew about my problem. Now Jack was one of the most accomplished speakers in the company. He'd stand up and talk to a crowd for hours, and he loved every minute of it. Just the thought of standing up made me perspire!

One morning I got an early phone call. It was Jack. His car had broken down on the highway, and he couldn't get to the office in time to speak to 130 sales prospects who would be waiting in the auditorium. I'd have to take his place!

"Isn't there someone else who can do it?" I asked Jack.

"Nope," was his answer. And there wasn't. We were in a bind. I would have to do the speech.

I certainly knew the presentation. I had seen Jack deliver it many times. It was just that I wasn't ready . . . although I now realize that I would never have been ready. So I got up on the platform and I gave the presentation. It was traumatic, but I made it. And I did it successfully. That ended my fear of public speaking, and it raised my self-esteem several notches.

I'm sure you've guessed the kicker. Jack told me later I had been set up. He hadn't had car trouble. He just knew that I needed a shove. He knew he could give that performance. But I had to prove it to myself, and he gave me that opportunity. Since then, I've enjoyed many years of public speaking.

3. Be a missionary

First you surround yourself with people. Then you build self-esteem in those people. Third, you help the people enrich their lives. The result is that you enrich yourself by helping others.

When you commit to helping people achieve success, they'll repay you with commitment, loyalty, energy, and high productivity—everything that it takes to be successful. Among my franchisees and business associates, there are numerous stories that would illustrate this point. But let me share just one with you. The story of how Lonnie & Joan Trevino got their own franchise.

In 1982, when I was very active in the recruiting end of our business, I was working with Lonnie Trevino, trying to get him into Rainbow. I worked with him for six months; it was always difficult to reach him, and even more difficult to bring to him the point of making a decision. At first, I thought it was just a cultural difference (Lonnie being a Mexican-American).

After he finally made the decision to sign up, I unearthed the real problem. His girlfriend Joan (now his wife) hadn't wanted to move from Houston to McAllen, Texas. Ultimately, they made the move and overcame all the financial obstacles that always seem to be the final test of your belief in owning your own business.

At the time Lonnie joined the organization, he was a route driver for Frito Lay. So—what has happened to him and Joan over the last ten years? They added another one of our franchises, Worldwide Refinishing Systems, to their service line. Lonnie is an international trainer working in Ireland, England, Spain, and Guatemala. They have built two successful businesses. In 1991, they sold their Rainbow license for $165,000, realizing a profit of $150,000. They are now expanding their Worldwide Refinishing franchise, increasing their income, and improving their quality of life.

Ask yourself: Where would Lonnie and Joan be today if they had *not* gone into their own business? The answer—delivering Fritos and struggling to make ends meet. As it stands, they are financially independent, international trainers who are free to do what they want. They are extremely happy. What's more, they belong to a family of 7,000 people and are welcomed in homes all over the world.

You can take people from all walks of life, with any level of education, and teach them to be experts in your industry within a short period of time. All you have to do is teach them to follow the system.

---

4. Follow the system

In franchising—as well as in other businesses—you can take people from all walks of life, with any level of education, and teach them to be experts in your industry within a short period of time. All you have to do is teach them to follow the system.

Ah, but does a system exist? Every business is operated by a system. Frequently the system is chaotic, with people floating around trying to make the business work. Those businesses almost always end in failure.

I don't care what kind of a business you start. If it's not a franchise, someone operates a similar business. Find people who are really successful operating a business like the one you hope to build, and then copy their system. They might not share this information with you, of course, particularly if you pose a competitive threat to them. Or they might want to charge you a fee for using their system. I wouldn't blame them for that. If it's a good system, it would be worth the price.

As I explained in the previous chapter, every good

franchise not only operates by a system; the system is recorded in an operations manual, and possibly also on video tape and audio cassettes. In our franchises there's no need to reinvent the wheel. Like any good franchisor, we've developed a system to show our people how to get the job done, profitably.

5. Reproduce

To grow and prosper in business, you must reproduce. Sometimes that means you've got to enlarge the physical capacity of your business, or merely bring in more business. It could also mean operating multi-units, or covering a larger territory. A restaurant owner, for example, might attract more customers by broadening the menu. If you've watched McDonald's through the years, you understand what I'm saying. Remember when McDonald's used to be known for inexpensive hamburgers, terrific French fries, and thick milkshakes? They still are, of course, but now you can buy breakfast at McDonald's. You can get a salad. Cookies. Low-fat yogurt. Even McPizza! McDonald's obviously has a need to attract more customers, and it has helped their franchise owners do so by broadening the menu.

Mailboxes Etc. is another good example. The company started out renting mail boxes. Today, Tony DeSio, the founder, oversees a worldwide chain of more than two thousand franchised outlets that not only rent mail boxes but also provide a variety of business and consumer services, including faxing, Western Union messages, U.P.S. deliveries, and so on. The company continues to reproduce, and I believe it will eventually open more than ten thousand units, becoming an institution in its industry.

6. Work your tail off

The sixth law of multiplication is the universal rule of success. It will multiply your wealth faster than anything I know. Without this rule, none of the other fives rules is worth much.

All of the successful business owners I know work more than forty hours a week. One day I figured out that I work an average of sixty-four hours a week. That means I've probably put in twenty-four more years of work than the average man my age. And that's one of my secret weapons of success. As Thomas Edison said, "There's no substitute for hard work."

I'm not any different from anyone else who wants to get ahead. I haven't done anything you can't do. So long as you're willing to work hard.

If you're already an entrepreneur, you know that building a business isn't a nine-to-five job. Moreover, since it's your own business you probably don't mind working those extra hours if it is profitable to you to do so.

These are people who work their tails off, and if you're willing to join them, you can anticipate your success in business.

If you work for a corporation, you've learned that the people who get ahead are usually the people who say good night from their desks when everyone else goes home. It's the person who works as long as it takes to get the job done, and then still puts in some extra time, perhaps planning for the next project. These are people who work their tails off, and if you're willing to join them, you can anticipate your success in business.

I'm not advising you to become a workaholic. Remember the Wheel of Life in Chapter Seven. Every life requires balance, including having fun. People get rich finding something they like to do, and then *doing* it. I'll tell you another one of my secrets, since I'm in that mode. To me, working *is* fun. I'm excited about what I do. If you are, too, then you'll be able to have fun while you work your tail off!

Summing up, let's review the Six Laws of Multiplication:

- *Law Number One:* People Are Power. Don't try to be a one-man band; it won't work. The power is in recruiting people to help you.
- *Law Number Two:* Build Self-esteem. Make sure your self-esteem is high, and then help your people build their self-esteem.
- *Law Number Three:* Be A Missionary. Enrich your life by helping your employees, associates, ven-

dors, and customers. You'll reap the harvest you sow.

- *Law Number Four:* Follow The System. Learn the rules of operating the business successfully. Follow those rules, and you'll prosper.
- *Law Number Five:* Reproduce. Keep growing. Don't be satisfied with the status quo. The bigger you build your operation, the greater your chances for making the big money.
- *Law Number Six:* Work Your Tail Off. Do whatever it takes to get the job done, and then do some more. It's called paying your dues.

These laws have worked for hundreds of my franchisees. They'll work for you too, if you make a commitment to them.

ACTION ITEM

Praise yourself today. It will build your self-esteem, and it will help you praise others more easily, which in turn, will help them build their self-esteem. So tell yourself, "You did a great job today."

Doing this might feel a little strange at first, but try it. For any little thing at all that you accomplish, congratulate yourself. Do it at least once today!

The P.I.P. Theory

Here's an effective image-building technique that I use in my life, and you can use it, too.

My P.I.P. Theory says, "Praise Is Power."

Have you ever ended a day by saying to yourself, "I didn't get anything done today!"

When you say that, even to yourself, you're lowering self-image. And as I've said before, a strong self-image is the key to success and happiness.

Let me show you how the P.I.P. Theory works.

One day one of my bookkeepers came into my

continued on next page

office to have me sign some checks. She came in slowly and slightly stooped over. After signing the checks, I said to her, "Your supervisor tells me you're doing a great job." She smiled, and when she left, I noticed that her whole posture had changed. She threw her shoulders back and walked briskly out of my office.

That's when I discovered that Praise Is Power.

Then I thought to myself, "Why don't I praise people more often?"

The answer: "Because I don't praise myself enough."

I decided to do an experiment of sorts during the next business day. I would praise myself. After completing each task during my day, I would find something good to say about what I had done, even if I hadn't completed the job to my complete satisfaction. At the end of that day, I felt great about myself.

As I became more aware of how this powerful process affected me, I knew that I could help other people feel better about themselves if I praised them. So I did. And guess what happened? People started praising me, too, making me feel all the better about myself. As I gave more praise, I received more praise!

Praise Is Power. Put the P.I.P. Theory to work for yourself and see what happens.

If you would like to receive a copy of the Praise Is Power poem, please call or write to me.

11.
The Money Test

"In the current banking climate, even if you're one of the bank's best customers, it's almost a waste of time to ask an American bank to support a new business venture with a loan."

"I believe you do what you've got to do, within the law and the bounds of morality."

"Money alone is not a good enough reason to take in a partner."

DON DWYER

Nearly everyone I meet thinks about starting a business. But most fail what I call "The Money Test."

Getting together the money that you'll need to start a business is a test that measures the height of your desire, the depth of your commitment, and the quality of your character. Whether you pass or fail the test, you'll find out a lot about your ability to handle rejection and disappointment, and—perhaps most importantly—your response to adversity.

Let me tell you a story about a man I'll call Frank. He was very excited about getting into a business of his own, and he had thought out all of the details, including a business plan. All that was missing was the start-up capital. He needed about $20,000, but he was sure he could get the capital from his local bank.

Frank had done a good job of preparing for business ownership. His business plan made sense, he had defined several short-term and long-term targets, his financial projections were reasonable, and he surely had the enthusiasm to get the job done. So he decided to visit his local bank and arrange for a loan. His family had been doing business with this bank for years, and he had obtained financing from this bank for his house and, through the years, several cars. He had a perfect credit rating with the bank, so he had every right to think that the bank would grant him a loan.

Why banks don't loan to entrepreneurs

When Frank met with the bank's loan manager, a man he had known for several years, the manager expressed some enthusiasm in Frank's projected business. He showed Frank how to complete an application for a loan, and when Frank returned with the completed application a couple of days later, the manager said it looked pretty good. The manager said he would submit the application to the bank's loan committee, and Frank should get a response within a few days.

Two weeks later, Frank was told by his "friendly banker" that his loan application was denied. The loan committee had said it wasn't interested in financing Frank's business. Shocked, disappointed, and depressed, that's when Frank came to see me. Almost overnight he had gone from a confident new entrepreneur to a man filled with self-doubt.

"Could it be," Frank wondered out loud, "that the bank knows something about my proposed business idea that I don't know? Or is there something wrong with my credit?"

It was neither of the above. I said to Frank, "Welcome to the world of banking in the land of free enterprise!"

If Frank's banker had been honest with him from the moment he set foot into the bank to apply for a loan, he would have told him that banks hardly ever lend money for new business ventures. If a customer has a $25,000 Certificate of Deposit in the bank and wants to borrow against it to start-up a business, the bank might go along with loaning the customer some of that money. Otherwise, in the current banking climate, even if you're one of the bank's best customers, it's almost a waste of time to ask an American bank to support a new business venture with a loan.

It used to be that if you had good credit, you could go to your local bank and borrow $2,500 to $25,000 or more on your signature. But not anymore. Even when you've got collateral, business financing from a bank is the ultimate jump-through-the-hoops exercise. Just when you think you've made it through the last hoop, the banker pops up another one!

Well, it's not really the local bank's fault. The Federal regulators have virtually stopped the flow of money that business people need to launch a new venture, or sustain an already-existing small business. The problem is in Washington, D.C., not in your community.

I've always found it curious that the same first-time entrepreneurs who are granted loans in Canada and England would be denied those loans in the United States. The Royal Bank of Canada frequently arranges loans through its New Venture Program, which it offers in cooperation with the government to encourage business start-ups. I've discovered that the Canadian banks are especially partial to franchise businesses because they know that at least 90 percent of the ventures will be successful.

The same is true in the United Kingdom. When my organization exhibits in a franchise trade show in England, loan officers from several of the major banks are there competing for business. They, too, like franchise enterprises. They understand that a loan to a new franchisee is a method of expanding their customer base. They also understand that small businesses frequently do grow into big businesses. Maybe the bankers in Canada and the U.K. know some things that bankers in the United States ought to take the time to learn!

But until then, as I told Frank, we've simply got to stop counting on our banking institutions to support us financially or emotionally if we want to be entrepreneurs. The last thing a first-time entrepreneur needs is to be discouraged and demoralized by a faceless bank loan committee.

Frank had to find other sources of financing—unconventional but legitimate sources that would be more painful than filling out a loan application but would nonetheless be a means to an end. And that's how I proceeded to help Frank.

It is at this point that many people give up their dream to own a business. When we talk about start-up capital, and what they might have to do to get it, they don't want to continue the process. And I don't encourage them because, frankly, those who can't stand up to this pressure will probably fail in business, where adversity is always waiting to give an entrepreneur a tumble. Frank wasn't going to give up, though. So I counseled him in some of the techniques that my franchisees and I have frequently used to obtain start-up and operating capital. Some of these techniques may work for you, too.

1. Commit to getting the money

I've experienced many setbacks and difficulties in my business career, but I've never been willing to live failure for even one minute. That's the attitude you *must* adopt if you're going to pass The Money Test. There's no stronger force than the will to win. Somehow you'll get the money you need to start your business.

The people who tell me, "I'll *try* to get the money together," rarely do. The people who grit their teeth and say, "*I will*," almost always do.

Once you've convinced yourself that you will be a successful entrepreneur, and you've got a solid plan to back up your ideas, you will do whatever must be done to keep moving forward.

Once you've convinced yourself that you will be a successful entrepreneur, and you've got a solid plan to back up your ideas, you will do whatever must be done to keep moving forward. And when that happens, people will respond to you favorably. The person who said "no" when you were doubtful about your business enterprise will now say "yes" because they recognize your sincerity, commitment, and certainty.

I thank a very determined woman, my mother, for instilling in me a value system that has made my life prosperous and had a profound impact on my family, my employees, and my franchise owners. My mother's philosophy was, "Don't do for others what they can and should do for themselves." She believed that too much help weakens people, and ultimately makes them resentful of your efforts.

I got that message beginning at an early age when I had to earn my own spending money. As a father, even though I had the money to give, I resisted the temptation to give my children what I knew they could earn for themselves. Had I made everything easy for my kids, just because I had plenty, there would have been short-term pleasure for me and long-term disappointments for them.

My son, Don, Jr., built his own home at age eighteen with his own money. He designed the house and supervised the crews. My twins, Darren and Douglas, ran a self-service car wash while they were still in high school. Daughters Debbie, Dina, and Donna all operated restaurants when they were in their teens. They did it on their own. I love watching these kids grow!

I've employed this same tough attitude with my employees and franchisees. And just as with my kids, I'm sure they're all better because of it.

I have, however, assigned counselors in my company to help people who have made the commitment to find the money they need to start up a business. These counselors are charged with the responsibility of instilling the philosophy of self-reliance and determination in the people they coach. And almost every day I hear of another new entrepreneur who has made the decision not to be denied a business for the lack of financing. As soon as that entrepreneur commits to getting the money, the money follows. This is such a common occurrence that it proves, in my mind at least, that there's a connection between commitment and obtaining capital.

2. List your resources

Most people have more resources than they think. They just don't realize it until they take an inventory. That's what I recommend you do: make a list of every item of value that you own. It doesn't matter what it is—your home, car, boat, jewelry, furs, land, collectibles, clothing, furniture, stocks, bonds—if it has value, list it.

Don't forget the stuff in the attic and the garage! Remember Aunt Ida's set of antique china. Your grandfather's stamp collection. Your old train set that your kids don't want. Almost every family, sooner or later, inherits something of value to a collector.

List it all! Decide what's not essential. What are you willing to sell? Then sell it. I've seen people who said, "We have no money" raise as much as $15,000 by selling off their inventory. Yes, it's painful to part with certain things. I still hate the fact that I had to sell my new convertible to buy my first business. But it was a worthwhile investment. Like me, you may have no other choice but to part with your dearest possessions.

3. *Mortgage the farm, or a piece of it*

Most financial advisors will tell you not to take a second mortgage on your home to start a new business. But you might have to do it. Many of my franchisees have done so. Banks or finance companies will generally lend 70 to 80 percent of the appraised, unmortgaged value of a home. If your home is worth $200,000, you can borrow up to 80 percent, or $160,000. If you have a $100,000 mortgage, that would give you $60,000 to invest in a business. Yes, it's risky. After all, you're placing your home on the line. Don't do it unless you're committed to succeeding in business, and even then, think about it again.

Maybe you won't have to mortgage the farm. Maybe, instead, you've got a life insurance policy you can borrow against. Consult your insurance agency and explore the opportunities.

Finally, do you have a retirement policy with cash value, or have you tucked away any IRA money? I once counseled a teacher who wanted to go into business. He had money in a retirement fund that would start paying him a monthly benefit when he reached age sixty. He had the option, however, of cashing in the entire fund for a lump sum payment, which he did. He figured he could put the money to work in his thirties, rather than wait for retirement.

Similarly, if you own IRAs, you can withdraw the money, although you'll have to pay certain penalties. The net cash should produce a higher return if you invest it in a successful business of your own.

I want to emphasize that all of these strategies are risky. Before you make a decision to put your home, your life insurance, or your retirement fund at risk, I recommend that you consult with your own financial advisors.

4. Use other people's money

One of today's fastest and most convenient sources of obtaining money is through the credit card. You probably already have at least one or more Master Cards, VISA, or other credit card which allow you to take cash advances. Should you do it? There was a time when I advised against it, but the credit card is now frequently one of your few means of obtaining cash. I believe you do what you've got to do, within the law and the bounds of morality.

You can use multiple credit card cash advances to obtain thousands, even tens of thousands, of dollars for start-up and operating capital. If your payment record is good, you can usually get your credit limit increased. You can even apply for additional credit cards at other banks.

If you borrow against your credit card, work extra hard to pay off the balances fast, because the interest rates are outrageous. But don't worry about paying extra interest—that money can be replaced, but time lost can never be made up.

While credit cards are one form of using other people's money, this approach also includes borrowing from family and friends. In fact, family and friends are your best sources for raising capital. Statistics show that 80 percent of all new businesses are financed with personal resources, including help from family and friends.

In business financing we're returning to the ethic of the pioneer days, when family and friends supported one another. It used to be that if you needed a barn, or a house, your family and members of your community got behind the effort and helped you. The Amish are the only people I know of today who still build barns for each other, but families and friends will still loan money. One of the advantages to this form of borrowing is that you can usually set up a flexible payment schedule, giving you some room to maneuver while you grow the business.

Your parents may have cash value in an insurance

policy they'd be willing to loan to you. They may have savings they'd be willing to tap for you, a collectible they'd be willing to let you sell. Other relatives with an interest in helping you get started in a business might give you a loan with little or no interest. The same is true of friends.

Certainly it's difficult to ask these people for money. Most people don't want to do it, and sometimes for good reasons. But many people don't want to do it because they're too proud. If that's your reason, then ask yourself this question: How would I feel if a family member or friend, someone I really cared about, asked me for a loan?

Chances are, you'd feel flattered. And you'd want to help, if you could. So don't "feel funny" about asking people for a loan. If you show them why you need the money, and they see you're committed to succeed, they'll probably want to play a part in your success.

When I bought my first business, I not only had to sell my convertible, I also had to borrow money from my bride-to-be *and* her family. That really put me on the line. It also really motivated me. I made a commitment to myself to pay them back faster than promised, and I did so, in just six months.

When you approach people you know to ask for money for a new business opportunity, there are some things you can do to give yourself greater confidence and to make it easier for them to agree to assist you. Make your approach professional. Show them your business plan. Explain why your opportunity is a good one. And offer to pay a better rate of interest than what they're getting from their savings account, CDs, or insurance policies. Then commit yourself to a reasonable payback arrangement.

Don't ask for help based on blood relationships or blind faith. Blood may be thicker than water, but when it comes to money, blood dilutes fast! Don't mix your relationship with the financial transaction. Put the deal in writing, and make it a legitimate business arrangement.

At the end of this chapter I've provided a detailed exercise that will help you prepare to make a loan presentation to family and friends (see page 138). It's the same presentation that we teach our prospective franchisees.

Getting started is the key

These techniques should help you get the money you need for your business enterprise. As I said, the techniques helped me. The money I raised by selling my car and borrowing from Terry (now my wife) and her family would be about $24,000 in today's dollars. With that start, I earned more than $1 million in less than ten years!

By the way, the same techniques helped Frank get started, too. He got his $20,000 by selling several of his possessions, including a boat, and borrowing money from his brother.

I can introduce you to any number of successful business owners who got started by borrowing money in a patchwork fashion from credit cards, family, and friends and put themselves under pressure to pay loans back quickly. What I cannot show you is a successful business owner who never got started!

You want to succeed in business? Then get started.

A word about partners

My advice is to borrow all the money you need and don't take in a partner—or even a long-term investor.

When I set out to buy my newspaper route, I discovered that I needed a little more money than I managed to borrow. So I convinced a friend who was in the real estate business to join me in my new opportunity as a full partner. Bad decision. My partner was unable to get himself out of bed in the morning. I soon found myself doing 90 percent of the work for 50 percent of the profits. Eventually I was able to buy him out.

I always thought of my decision to go into a partnership as a "semi-mistake." It would have been more difficult, but not impossible, to get started in business without my partner's money. But I lost money in the deal.

I also learned a lesson about the high price of a partner's money. Money alone is not a good enough reason to take in a partner.

Of course, as you may recall from chapter 2, I did enter a second partnership in my business career, when I couldn't convince the owner of Guarantee Carpet to let me buy his business. That partnership was a "semi-mistake," too. It didn't work and it cost me plenty, but the adversity of that experience motivated me to build the huge organization that I now own.

If you begin your business with patchwork borrowing, and you don't have to include a partner or an investor, I believe you'll be better off. In fact, after a year or two in business, if you've established a good track record, you may be able to replace the patchwork of loans with a start-up loan from a conventional bank (although don't hold your breath) or with help from the U.S. Small Business Administration. With some form of conventional financing, you'll be able to pay off your relatives, friends, and credit cards, reorganize your debt service, and own your business 100 percent.

A final word about banks

My earlier indictment of the banking industry may have been a little rough. I don't take a word of it back, however. Our bankers have a lot to learn about supporting business ventures. Fortunately, some bankers agree with me. And those are the bankers who get my business.

A business needs a bank, don't get me wrong. You can't build a fortune without using borrowed money. So in spite of all my previous cautions about bank borrowing, I'm now going to tell you that it will someday be necessary, with few exceptions, to borrow money from a bank. However, the kind of borrowing that I'm now talking about, and under the conditions that I'm setting out, is not difficult to achieve.

It's important for you, as an entrepreneur, to establish banking relationships as quickly as possible, and to make them positive, successful experiences.

If you become known as trustworthy and credit-worthy, if you pay your debts on time, live up to your commitments, and spend your money cautiously, you will soon attract financial institutions that want to do business with you.

As you build a reputation as a successful business person, you establish a solid foundation that supports your financial security. If you become known as trustworthy and credit-worthy, if you pay your debts on time, live up to your commitments, and spend your money cautiously, you will soon attract financial institutions that want to do business with you. In fact, you're just what they're looking for!

At some point a bank wants you to take its money; otherwise, the bank can't make a profit. The problem is always that your friendly banker has to be sold by you *first* before the bank will part with its merchandise!

Begin early to earn the trust of a banker, even two or three bankers. When I'm bank shopping, I use the Yellow Pages of my phone directory. I plan to visit every bank in town, providing that it's convenient to my business and makes business loans. Often, by the way, the best bank for me is not the one closest to my business. Nor is it the first one or two that come to mind.

When you go into the bank, ask the receptionist to introduce you to the manager, or to the loan officer who is most aggressive about securing new customers. When you meet this person, make it clear that you're looking for a long-term banking relationship, some place to deposit your money and keep your accounts. That's music to a banker's ears. Once the banker gets to know you and sees that you're operating a successful business, the bank may very well want to help fund the continued growth of your business.

However, before any decisions are made about where you'll open an account, ask the manager or loan officer to tell you how the bank can help the small business person. Take notes during your interview. This not only shows that you care enough to keep records of your conversation, it will also help you compare notes from conversations with other bankers.

Once you decide to open an account at a particular bank, start building your relationship with the banker. Give him (or her) your business plan. Show him brochures and newspaper articles that explain your business. Also give him your financial statements and your personal balance sheet. You can get these items from your accountant.

Paperwork is very important to bankers. Notice how much paperwork they create and how much of it they pass from one desk to another. Put some effort into your paperwork before you turn it over to your banker. Be sure it's accurate and neat. If it's not, the banker may begin to think that if you're careless with your paperwork, you're also careless with the way you conduct your business, including your loan payments. Look, banks are easily deterred from loaning money. Don't give the banker any reason not to help you!

It's also important to let your banker see you *at the bank*. I know this sounds trivial, but it's important. One of the things I don't like about Automated Teller Machines is that they prevent us from personal contact with our bankers.

I encourage all my franchisees to go into the bank to make deposits. Give the banker a big wave and a smile. If the banker isn't busy, stop by and brag a little bit about your business.

Make it a point to keep the banker informed at least once a month. And don't hold back the bad news. Share it. Seek the banker's advice. Involve the banker in your business. An added benefit is that you get the services of an unpaid Vice President of Finance!

What will you need to get a replacement loan from a bank to pay off your patchwork borrowing? The following:

- A successful track record, completely documented with current financial statements
- A detailed business plan showing how the financing will reduce your total monthly debt service and/or other costs, and facilitate business growth
- A good business credit history, with references
- Good personal credit

My franchisees often report their surprise to me when, after a few months of building a relationship with a bank, they're offered a loan. That's the way it should happen. Banks are looking for *proven* business people. But bankers are like parachutists. They won't jump unless they have a backup chute strapped to their chests, just in case the primary chute doesn't work. So the banker will ask for collateral. That's the backup chute. It's something they can seize and sell—or someone they can squeeze—in the event that a loan goes bad.

I suppose all of this is reason enough to say there's no

sense grumbling about bankers not taking risks. They don't earn their keep by taking risks. They earn it by making safe loans. But I'm going to grumble anyway, particularly in favor of banks supporting franchise businesses. We urgently need our banks to lend a helping hand to the franchise business community. Otherwise the banks are doing more to discourage the American Dream than to encourage people to live it, and to profit from it.

End of editorial.

And the end of another chapter.

Once you pass The Money Test, you'll be looking at a different person when you stand in front of a mirror. You will have uncovered persuasive abilities, self-discipline, patience, persistence, and powers you didn't know you possessed.

ACTION ITEM

Today, right now, I want you to take an inventory of your household possessions. This is an assignment you should complete even if you're not looking for money to start a business. You need this information for insurance companies, and for your personal financial statement. Go through every room and list your possessions. Go to the attic and look around. Do the same in the garage and the basement. Take an inventory of everything you see, whether you want to sell it or not. Once your list is completed you can sit down and analyze the contents. Maybe there are some items that you ought to sell. Maybe there are some valuable items that are worth substantial money. An ad in the newspaper, or a series of garage sales, might be all you need to do to raise some capital.

HOW TO ASK RELATIVES & FRIENDS FOR A LOAN

The purpose of this exercise is to give you an organized and proven process to follow when enlisting the help of relatives and friends to finance your business start-up.

1. State purpose of your visit.

"_____, I've made a decision to go into business for myself. I would like to ask for your help. *I'm not asking for advice.* I've researched and evaluated the business thoroughly. I need your financial support."

2. Sell yourself.

"I think I am worth investing in, and here are some reasons why . . . ."

You could review any of the following which support your statement of worth:

- Past successes
- Honors and awards
- Proof of character

Then ask, "Is this the kind of person you'd like to invest in?"

3. Sell your business opportunity.

Recap the information you know about the business. If you're investing in a franchise business, for example, conclude by saying:

"_____ Company is the best of its kind. They support more than _____ other franchisees. I want to become part of this dynamic company. I have the desire. They have the know-how, which they're willing to teach me. I am willing to work hard. They will work with me. I have the confidence and the belief that I can be very successful in this business. With your help, and the help of _____ Company, I can do it."

4. Project your sales and income.

Your business plan should include a projection of sales, and your income, for at least one year. Share that information. Also, break down your numbers to show your sales level per month, and for one year; your profit per month, and for one year; and the value of your business after one year.

5. State how much money you need.

"_____, I need to raise $_____. Would you help me? I'd like to ask you to invest $_____ in me. Would you do that?"

6. Review the payback method.

"_____, I'd like to pay you back over _____ years, at _____ interest. The first year I'd like to pay you $_____, plus interest every 90 days. The second year I'd like to pay you $_____, plus interest every ninety days. Thereafter, I'll pay you $_____ every _____."

continued on next page

7. Cite the benefits to both prospect and lender

"_____, there will be several benefits to both of us if you help me." Then review:

Benefits to lender:
- "You will be helping me succeed. This is my dream to own my own business."
- "I'll pay you a better interest rate than you're now earning elsewhere."

Benefits to prospect:
- "I'll be getting started in business sooner, rather than later, so I can start earning money now."
- "I'll be able to build a secure future for my family."

If you're investing in a franchise opportunity, you can add:
- "I'll be associated with successful, positive people who can help me make my business very successful."

8. Close

Depending on your circumstances, and the kind of business you're starting, you may use one of several different closes:

- "I have asked the _____ Company to reserve a place for me in their next training program, which begins _____. With your help, I will be able to keep my commitment to attend that training session."
- "Is the interest amount that I stated, and the payback method, satisfactory to you?"
- "Have I left out anything that you'd like to know? Is there any other information that would help you make the decision to help me?"

12.
How to Build and Manage an Outstanding Business

"I made up my mind that I would re-earn my right to be president of my company every day. One of the ways I do that is by planning my day."

"I'm all for making big, exciting, very specific promises, and delivering more than was promised. By doing so, your business will surpass 99 percent of all other businesses."

"There are two ways to manage your business: like a firefighter or like a traffic cop."

DON DWYER

One thing about business that should not surprise anyone, but often does, is that the business owner's major challenge is getting, satisfying, and retaining customers. Many would-be and new business owners visualize themselves sitting behind their desks or store counters . . . stocking shelves and playing with merchandise displays . . . chatting with customers . . . counting money . . . and somehow enjoying plenty of business, which they assume magically appears. Well, it just doesn't happen that way.

As a business owner, you're going to have to get up, get out, and go get your customers. That means you'll have to see people, sell people, and serve people.

Every business works that way, even big business. But the entrepreneur has the edge over big business when it comes to winning customers, because big business is usually restricted to attracting customers through location and mass advertising. Basically, big business has to buy its customers. And that's costly, because big business will frequently lose money on the first transaction with a new customer, hoping to make a profit on repeat business from that same customer.

Big business was never designed to facilitate person-to-person marketing. But that technique is how successful entrepreneurs build profitable businesses.

As an entrepreneur, you don't have to depend on the very best and the most expensive retail location in town. You don't have to depend on costly mass advertising campaigns. You depend on *yourself*, and on the people who join your team. You use the most effective kind of marketing that exists, person-to-person marketing: meeting people, creating rapport with people, building relationships with people, influencing people, and servicing them as customers.

Service matters most

One of the secrets to building a successful business is service. I'm not talking just about service businesses but all kinds of businesses. Even retail outlets provide a service in the way they treat their customers and in the way they de-

---

The first big question you should ask yourself when you begin to build your business is, "What can I do, or provide, to satisfy all of my customers so that they'll share their excitement for my business with everyone they know?"

sign their stores for ease of shopping.

There's simply no substitute for doing a top-quality job, one that's so good your customers will be pleasantly surprised and won't stop talking about your business to their neighbors and friends. So the first big question you should ask yourself when you begin to build your business is, "What can I do, or provide, to satisfy all of my customers so that they'll share their excitement for my business with everyone they know?" When you get this force working in your favor, your business can't help but succeed.

Earl Nightingale suggested that if a business person would spend just thirty minutes every morning doing nothing but thinking of ways to be of better service to customers, that business person would never again worry about attracting more customers. I agree! Yet it's so easy to get stuck with the "busyness" of your business that you can lose sight of what really makes it successful. No matter how busy you get, never stop analyzing how you can use your energies and resources to take better care of your customers. In turn, they'll take care of your business.

Through the years we've been able to demonstrate the power of service to our franchisees. It arrives in the form of letters from customers. For example, I received a letter from a prominent real-estate broker in one of our franchise territories. It said, "We now know that if anyone can get [a stain] out [of a carpet], Greg can." The real estate agent was talking about one of our franchisees, who had apparently removed a stubborn stain. That's a problem our franchisees face every day. By taking care of such problems quickly and professionally, our franchisees frequently amaze their customers. In the case of the real estate agent, our franchisee benefited from countless referrals. Think of all the prospective carpet cleaning and dyeing customers a real-estate agent meets in a week! One satisfying job can translate into tens of thousands of dollars in revenue for a business.

I received another letter from a customer who praised one of our franchisees for speedy service in an emergency situation. This customer's father had died, and his mother was upset not only about the death of her spouse but also because she was embarrassed to have people come to her home to offer their condolences when her carpets were dirty. It may not seem like much of a problem to many people, given the circumstances, but the dirty carpets mattered to this lady.

When our franchisee heard about the situation, he rearranged his schedule, rushed to the woman's home, and literally finished the carpets as people were arriving at the front door. From the praising content of the customer's letter, there was simply no smarter, more effective marketing move that franchisee could have made that day!

Believe me. Excellence in service is the most powerful marketing strategy of all.

When you coast, you soon roll to a stop!

One of the business values in my organization is that everyone must re-earn her position in the company every day. Let me explain why.

During my tenure with SMI, I worked with a number of companies, mostly small to mid-sized businesses, some of them earning annual sales in the hundreds of millions of dollars. My objective was to help these companies implement management training and development programs. Invariably I would meet a manager, or another employee, who had been with a particular company for many years and was "retired in place." Some of these people actually believed they had earned the right *not* to work. They were coasting. And you know what happens when you coast. Eventually you'll roll to a dead stop.

Realizing this, I made up my mind that I would re-earn my right to be president of my company every day. One of the ways I do that is by planning my day. And in that plan I make sure to include a project so valuable and important for my organization that if I weren't already the president, I'd be promoted to that position for having accomplished the project.

This is the challenge that I put on my proverbial plate every morning, and I intend to continue doing so as long as I sit in this office. I expect the executives in my organization (and those who want to become executives) to re-earn their positions every day, too.

Coasting frequently occurs in family businesses. What is it they say about family businesses? "From rags to rags in three generations." It's easy to see how that happens. The first generation knows poverty and works hard to pull out of it. The second generation is used to being comfortable, and once they inherit the business they do little to expand it. They coast. And by the time the business arrives in the hands of the third generation, it has almost stopped working.

I've seen franchisees coast, too. Like those managers who had retired on the job, business owners can easily develop the attitude that they've earned the right not to work. After all, they own the business! And besides, the business has already reached a certain level of activity and will continue to do so. They think. So they stop going out and seeing people, selling people, and servicing customers. They relax, satisfied with the business at hand. They coast. And soon, the business stops working.

I tell my franchisees that business owners need to re-earn their positions every day. And I'm sending you the same message!

How to get a customer

Getting customers is a process. The process differs for every business, and it must be tailor-made for the business. But once the process is developed, anyone can learn it, regardless of the kind of business.

Following are several marketing steps you can use to create a marketing plan that will attract customers to your business.

1. Think of customers as human beings

The first step to getting customers is to separate yourself from the big, impersonal companies. You can do that by refusing to think of customers as nameless and faceless, or worse, as numbers or statistics. Every customer is a person, with fears, worries, needs, desires, busy schedules, and all sorts of concerns.

2. Profile your customer

Once you realize that customers are humans, you then need to create a profile of your customer. Who will do business with you? Who will buy your products and services? Why will they do so? What benefits will they seek from your products and services?

Get into the mind of your customer, or prospective

customer. What makes him tick? What makes him *need* your product or service? Does he know he needs your product or service? Or will you have to create that need for him?

Understanding your customers' needs is paramount to winning their business. I can't emphasize it enough. The business person who can successfully figure out what's going on in the customer's mind, and see the business from the customer's point of view, can win the customer's business.

3. Position your business

You must position your product or service in a way that will satisfy the customer's needs. That's not the same as telling your prospective customers—via advertising—what your products will do or what your service will provide. That's a common mistake among businesses, and it accounts for billions of dollars wasted in all forms of advertising.

It's much more effective to show the prospective customer how your product or service satisfies their needs. And that may require some creative thinking on your part. However, it's easier to do if you understand the customer's reasons for buying a particular product or service.

Let me give you an example. Carpet cleaning is a service business that cleans carpets. That's obvious. A customer who has soiled carpets will hire a carpet cleaner to clean those carpets. That's obvious, too. There are lots of soiled carpets in the world—in homes, in offices, in restaurants, in hotels and motels—so people in the carpet cleaning business ought to be able to stay busy.

But the fact is, they don't. Lots of people who get into this business, particularly on their own, fail miserably. One of the reasons they fail is that they don't properly position their businesses in the minds of customers. They assume that all they've got to do is advertise their service, and people who want their carpets cleaned will call them. That doesn't work.

People with soiled carpets frequently want their carpets cleaned, that's true. However, they know it's not very difficult to clean a carpet. Many people, in fact, clean their own carpets, or they've done so in the past. There's no mystery to the business. Oh sure, there are better cleaning chemicals, better equipment, better processes. And stains are tough to remove, if you don't know how. But all in all, people understand this about carpet cleaning.

They also believe that one carpet cleaner is about as good as the next. Just look at the advertising. They all tell you they're fast, effective, and inexpensive. So if a customer picks up the Yellow Pages and looks under carpet cleaning, it's simply a matter of pointing to one of the ads and dialing the phone to get a carpet cleaner. A lot of businesses attract customers this way. Frequently, the business with the largest ad gets the biggest share of the marketplace.

But that's surface marketing. The smart marketer penetrates the surface. And that's what separates the profitable businesses from those that merely stay busy.

The smart marketer knows that people don't hire a carpet cleaning company just because they want their carpets cleaned. There are other, more important needs they want the company to fulfill. For example, home beautification is an important need among carpet cleaning customers. Rainbow Carpet Cleaning & Dyeing franchisees can fulfill this need among their customers better than any of their competitors. That's because our franchisees tint carpets. We also do designer dyeing of carpets.

Other needs include fast service, security—knowing that the cleaners are trustworthy—and professional work. The business that communicates that it will fulfill those needs will attract the customers. Therefore, it's important to position your company to meet the customers' needs.

4. Ask for the business.

You can't be timid, humble, or hesitant if you're going to build a successful business. You've got to go out and persuade customers to buy from you. There are many ways of accomplishing this objective, and there are many books, audio tapes, and seminars that will guide you through this process. I recommend that you read the series of *Guerilla Marketing* books by Jay Levinson, and *Positioning: The Battle For Your Mind*, by Al Ries and Jack Trout.

How to satisfy a customer

Promises made, promises kept, promises surpassed. To attract a customer, you will make certain promises. And I'm all for making big, exciting, very specific promises, and delivering more than was promised. By doing so, your business will surpass 99 percent of all other businesses.

All you've really got to do to stay ahead of most businesses is keep your promises. You don't even have to deliver more than you promise. If you just do what you say you'll do, customers will appreciate you. Surely as a consumer you've noticed that promises don't mean much anymore in business. The printer "promised" to have our job done on Tuesday, but he "had a problem" so it won't be ready until Thursday. The airline "promised" to get you to Houston by 7 p.m., but they "had a mechanical" so the flight was delayed an hour. The hotel "promised" you a wake-up call at 6:15, but they "forgot." The dry cleaner, the restaurant, the car dealer—they all make promises, and they don't deliver.

As an entrepreneur, if you treat your promises as meaningful, binding, life-or-death contracts, your reputation, and your business, will benefit enormously. Your customers wouldn't dream of calling anyone else for the products or services you sell them.

Now, if you really want to stick it to your competition, just surpass your promises. Do everything agreed to and then one thing more. Whatever you promised, do it better or faster than the customer expected. Your customers will be *amazed*. And your business will rank among the top 1 percent.

There's another way to satisfy a customer, although nothing replaces promises made, promises kept, promises surpassed. This is something in addition. You should *value* your customers.

Let your customers know that you genuinely appreciate their business. Send them personal, handwritten thank-you notes. Call to make sure they're happy with their purchase. From time to time, send them important information that relates to their business. Send them birthday cards, holiday greetings, and gifts. Let your customers know—frequently—that you have not forgotten them, and that you look forward to serving them again.

Obviously, none of this is revolutionary. Yet very few business owners show their customers that they value them. That's why it sends a powerful message any time you do it!

Managing your business

You want to be a firefighter or a traffic cop?

"What's that got to do with managing my business?" you ask.

Well, let me tell you. There are two ways to manage your business: like a firefighter or like a traffic cop.

What does a firefighter do? Puts out fires, of course. And that's what you'll do as a fire-fighting manager. You'll oversee a business that's perpetually in turmoil. There will always be a fire to put out. A crisis, a problem, an emergency, a last-minute decision.

Now if you like that kind of energy-zapping management style, you'll find plenty of role models. Most businesses are managed by firefighters, many of them burned out. If you're an employee, perhaps your boss is a firefighter. So you know what I mean. By the way, you can always tell who the firefighters are because their businesses run them. They don't run their businesses.

Traffic-cop managers run their businesses. They stand (or sit) poised at the center of the business, where they can oversee all the action from every direction, anticipate problems, and move with the flow of traffic. They know when to speed up the business. They know when to slow it down. If there's an emergency, a crisis, a problem, the traffic-cop manager dispatches people to handle it. Meanwhile, the traffic-cop manager keeps the business moving.

I don't know about you, but I want to make my life as easy and enjoyable as possible, and that includes how I manage my business. I don't want to be controlled by my business. I want to control my business. I want my business to give me the freedom to do the things that make me happy. Putting out fires definitely isn't my idea of having a good time. If it's yours, I recommend you go to your local firehouse and fill out an application!

It's not so easy to become a traffic-cop manager, although the job looks easy. There's a good reason for that. Remember in an earlier chapter I said that one of the benefits of investing in a franchise is that the franchisor will teach you a *system* for operating the business successfully?

(This is not the same as the Success System described in chapter 4. This is a specific system for operating a business.) The traffic cop manager works by a system. Even when an unexpected crisis occurs, there's a system for handling it.

The firefighting manager, on the other hand, doesn't have a system. Worse yet, the firefighter can neither predict nor control the fire. You never know for sure what a blazing fire is going to do. It can destroy an entire block in minutes. So no matter how hard the firefighting manager tries to control the business, the business has a power of its own, and that power can be destructive.

It's so much simpler to operate by a system. Whether or not you invest in a franchise, I recommend that you manage your business like the traffic cop, with a system. And I don't mean just a time-management system, though that's part of it. I'm talking about a total operating system for your business. It includes a departmental flow chart, the assignment of responsibilities, job descriptions, company policies and procedures, action plans for completing jobs, standards by which your work will be evaluated, a plan for communications, and much more.

"Wait a minute," you say. "I'm not thinking about building a major corporation. I'm thinking about running a business out of my home."

Doesn't matter! You still need a system by which you can operate the business. You still need to know what must be done and who's going to do it, on what time schedule and by what standards. If you're both employer and employee, that's all the more reason for you to establish a system by which you can make the business operate efficiently, effectively, and profitably. Otherwise, I assure you, the business will run you, if not ruin you.

If you don't buy someone's system, as a franchisee, for example, or model someone's system, you'll discover

---

People who go into business independently, without a system, sometimes not even realizing that they need a system, will spend years trying to figure out how to make their business work. Sometimes it's too late when they figure it out.

that it takes time, and trial and error, to develop a system. And it's costly. People who go into business inde- pendently, without a system, sometimes not even realizing that they need a system, will spend years trying to figure out how to make their business work. Sometimes it's too late when they figure it out.

Again, I was one of the fortunate people. Even before I invested in the SMI franchise, I figured out the impor- tance of managing by a system. I've always had a lot of projects in the works at any one time. So while I was build- ing my newspaper distribution business, I was going to college, and then I also got involved in the entertainment business. I needed a system to make everything work.

When I joined SMI, they taught me their system, and I in turn taught the system to my sales reps. We were also teaching management systems to our clients. So manage- ment-by-system became a priority to me.

You can bet that I operate by a system today. It's much different from the systems I had ten, twenty, and thirty years ago, but my responsibilities are different today. And a system should always support your role or responsibili- ties within your business.

Today, for example, I have thirteen key executives who are responsible for the day-to-day operations of my organization. Each of them operates by a system, of course, as does everyone in our company. Every year we establish :argets for our business, and each department is responsi- ble for doing its part to turn those targets into realities. Our system defines the role of everyone in the organization, in- cluding the president, and explains to them how their work will be evaluated, when it will be evaluated, and how they will be compensated.

My primary role is to manage the thirteen key execu- tives and make sure that they keep our organization on track. To accomplish these responsibilities, I've established this system:

- I select the best executives. They must be skilled professionals, but more importantly, they must be- lieve in the company's mission. Most of them come up from the ranks. In effect, they really pro- mote themselves.

- I conduct a monthly executive committee meeting where the seven managers report their progress to each other, making themselves accountable for their responsibilities. This also serves as a meeting to share ideas and to build our team.
- I conduct a monthly luncheon meeting with the management team of each division, or department. During that time we review the department's activities and progress.
- I developed an internal reporting system for communicating with my managers, making certain that we're all paying attention to the important details of the business.
- I meet monthly with my chief financial officer to review the company's budgets and financial statements.
- I make myself accessible to everyone in the organization. I will discuss important issues with people, sometimes challenge them or force them to make a decision. I always support them. Coach them. And make sure that we're all living up to the values of the organization.

With this system in place and operating, I now have the ability to grow my organization in many different directions. The structure for success exists. All I need to do is add the people!

One more important point about using my system, or any system. It doesn't prevent emergencies, crises, and problems. They still occur in my business, as they will in every business. But the system minimizes these occurrences through good planning. When they do occur, they're most likely caused by circumstances that we could not control, and the system is built to accommodate them.

Systems are powerful. Use one to operate your business!

Breaking your business out of a slump

At some point, even after you've implemented a system and it's working, you're going to wake up and realize that your business is smack in the middle of a sales slump. You weren't coasting, either. It just happened. And when it does, you've got to do something about it. Here's my formula for breaking your business out of a slump.

Change your focus

Acknowledge that sales have dropped off. Then, don't dwell on the fact. Instead, start to analyze everything about your business—the advertising, marketing, promotion, sales methods. Get a handle on what you've done in the past that's worked, and what you are not doing now.

Stop blaming

When business isn't going well, it's a common practice to blame it on someone, or something. Don't bother. Blame won't fix the problem!

Ask what can be done

This *will* fix the problem. There is always *something* that can be done, and the faster you get to it, the better. In most businesses you can counteract a slump with a promotion to past and present customers. In most businesses there is something that can be done to solicit new customers quickly. Get your pen, pad, and brains and start making a possibility list.

Set up new targets

Take the best ideas and frame them as new targets. If your idea is to contact previous customers with a "special offer," set up the targets to accomplish that project. For example, you might decide to complete fifteen telephone calls every day to previous customers, telling them about your new offer.

Make new commitments

Commit to those new targets. Take them very seriously. Get excited about them. Announce them!

Get into action, do it!

Sitting around worrying, whining, stewing, obviously isn't going to resolve your sales slump. It's up to you to make things happen. You've done it before. There's no question that you can do it again.

Your competitive edge

What happens when the economy sours, or your competition comes on strong, or you get caught by some other surprise? Hey, it's going to happen. That's part of being in business.

However, if you take an active role in satisfying your customers, you'll gain a competitive edge over most other businesses and over any circumstances that may occur. When you keep promises, and you surpass promises, you're reaching the highest possible levels of excellence in business. When you nurture relationships with customers and you meet their needs, you're heads above the rest of the crowd.

The strengths of these advantages combined provides you with so much power that the economy, the competition, and other troublesome external factors seem irrelevant!

ACTION ITEM

Operating a business by a system is so important that I can't emphasize it enough. I want you to read a book that addresses this issue. It's called *The E Myth* by Michael Gerber, and you can order it through your bookstore, or perhaps find it at the library. This is a revolutionary book! It's easy to read, full of good information, and indispensable to anyone who's starting a business or already operating a business. Get a copy today, and read it as soon as you've finished *Target Success*.

13.
Emotional Mastery

"What did you not accomplish because fear had a grip on you?"

"We learn our fears, so we can unlearn them. Whatever we create, we can change."

"Eliminate one fear before you move to the next. Keep in mind that you didn't learn your fears overnight and you won't make them disappear overnight."

"No one has a corner on making good decisions."

DON DWYER

How to master the four negative emotions that undermine opportunity

Four disempowering emotions challenge us every day, and they are the four emotions that all too often yank opportunity right out from under a well-intentioned, deserving person. I'm talking about fear, worry, anger, and guilt. People who know how to face these emotions head-on continue moving toward the completion of their target dreams. Those who don't know how become slaves to these emotions. Challenged by one or a combination of the four emotions, people who haven't mastered them lose control, and then they may lose hours, days, sometimes even months before getting back on track.

As an entrepreneur, you won't be able to avoid fear, worry, anger, and guilt. In fact, it's unrealistic to think you won't face at least one or two of these emotions every day. And they can zap your energy. But not if you learn how to master them. To do so, you've got to understand how they work, why they're dangerous, and then how successful people master them. By the way, I have found that the worst of the four is fear. Beat it, and you can almost always master the other three.

Target: Fear

Remember when you were a kid and you knew for a fact that a hungry, ugly monster hid under your bed or in your closet? Fear is our earliest memory of a negative emotion. It's basic to the human condition. In fact, we are born with two fears: falling and loud noises. Then we spend the rest of our lives developing all sorts of others.

Many of our greatest writers, thinkers and statesmen talked about fear. The Roman philosopher and statesman Seneca wrote, "If we let things terrify us, life will not be worth living." The Duke of Wellington said, "The only thing I am afraid of is fear." Philosopher Bertrand Russell wrote, "To conquer fear is the beginning of wisdom." And at his inauguration in 1933, Franklin Delano Roosevelt told America, "The only thing we have to fear is fear itself."

Take a moment and think back through the last five years. What did you fear? What did you not accomplish because fear had a grip on you? Did you miss any opportunities because you were afraid?

What if you had lived those years free of fear? How would life have been different? What opportunities would you have said "yes" to instead of "no"? What would your life be like today had you lived the past five years without fear?

An elderly woman was showing her grandchildren and friends one of her scrapbooks and she came to a series of photographs from a vacation many years earlier in Mexico. One of the grandchildren asked, "What do you remember most about that vacation?"

Suddenly, the woman's voice turned to sadness. "I remember how much fun everybody else had going up in the air, parasailing, and I wish I hadn't been too afraid to go up, too."

Ah, the opportunities we miss in life because of fear. If only we learned how to harness fear, and turn it into power!

Most of the time the people closest to us seem determined to hold us back. Why? There are many reasons. They fear they'll lose us when we become successful.

We learn our fears, so we can unlearn them. Whatever we create, we can change. We learn fears from parents, teachers, friends, relatives, and, surely, television. You'd think the people closest to us would encourage us to seek greater success in life. In the unusual case, that's true. But most of the time the people closest to us seem determined to hold us back. Why? There are many reasons. They fear they'll lose us when we become successful. They're jealous. They're transferring their own fears, confusing their state of fear with wisdom. They're acting out of ignorance. Whatever their motives, they are usually well-intentioned, but they instill fears in very subtle ways.

"But, Jim, are you sure you want to give up your secure job right now?" your father, mother, or friend will say in a doubtful voice. "The economy's certainly not very good. Are you sure you're ready to live without a weekly paycheck? What'll happen if your business doesn't do well? You might not get paid much. Do you really know what you're doing?"

These are the words that trigger fear. Images of failure, poverty, looking foolish, and so on pop up in our minds. And suddenly we can't make a decision. We can't move. Or we change our minds and keep the secure job. All the while, we're fighting ourselves internally, yearning for a breakthrough. But once fear takes over, we're finished.

I see this all the time. People make the decision to go into business until their relatives gang up and, under the guise of "saving" them, scare them into changing their minds. Instead of saving you, your relatives and friends can push you back into your tiny box and slam the lid!

But not if you don't let them. How do you do that? *By believing in yourself.* That's the antidote to fear.

Remember Robert Tunmire, the high-school dropout who came to work for me? I told his story in chapter 3. Robert's family told him the opportunity we offered him was too good to be true. It wasn't malicious. The family's attitudes stemmed from their own environment. Robert's father had been taught by his father to play it safe. His attitude was, "Don't get your hopes up too high." Robert's father, in turn, taught Robert to look for the gimmick if the deal looked good.

When Robert started paying attention to success, and to the idea that success principles could be learned and used by anyone, it was like throwing a lighted match on a gasoline spill!

One of Robert's first targets was to make more money than his father. He wasn't being hateful. He wanted his father's approval. And in a short period of time, he proudly showed his parents a paycheck for a larger sum than his father had ever earned at one time. Wouldn't you know that instead of praising him, Robert's father cautioned him about the lack of stability of a business that would pay someone that kind of money so quickly!

Undaunted, Robert continued working, all the while building belief in himself. During this time he was reading books and listening to tape libraries. He changed emotionally. And eventually, even his parents noticed it. In fact, Robert convinced his parents to put up their furniture as loan collateral so he could borrow $6,000 to buy his own business!

It took him six months to build that business, and then he sold it for a $25,000 profit. Robert bought, built, and sold other businesses, and ultimately accepted an executive position at our home office.

Robert Tunmire, voted "least likely to succeed" by almost everyone but himself, has never made less than $80,000 a year since his first year in his own business! He now believes that he will always win. If you develop the same attitude, I'm sure you too can succeed in business without being stopped by fear.

While nothing substitutes for the right attitude in the mastering of fear, there's something more you can do.

Here's an exercise that will clarify your fears and help you gain control over them.

List them. Writing out your fears in black and white is absolutely necessary if you're going to confront them. Listing fears, like dreams, is a way of validating them. No one's going to see your list, so be honest. Make the list complete. Whatever your fears, list them. These fears may include fear of poverty, fear of change, fear of meeting new people, fear of public speaking, fear of being laughed at, fear of heights, fear of looking stupid, fear of success, and so on.

Fear of success? Oh, yes. So many of us have been down for so long that we're afraid to be on top. We don't know what it would be like up there, and we fear the unknown. Could we handle it? As long as we nurture our fear of success, we'll never have to find out.

Go ahead, make your list now:

Here's what I fear:

_____

_____

_____

_____

_____

Now, prioritize your list. Put your worst fear at the top of the list. Then rank the fears in descending order, with your smallest fear at the bottom of the list.

My fears prioritized:

_____

_____

_____

_____

_____

Beginning with your lowest-prioritized fear, the one that frightens you least, list the actions that you could take to eliminate this fear. Work on only one fear at a time. Eliminate one fear before you move to the next. Keep in mind that you didn't learn your fears overnight and you won't make them disappear overnight.

Actions to eliminate my fear of _____ :

_____

_____

_____

_____

_____

Depending on the number of fears you've listed, and the emotional depth of those fears, you may need to use this process for several months, or several years. What I can tell you, however, is that the process works.

When I listed my fears some years ago, I realized that I was afraid of getting too close to people. I didn't know how to get to know them, how to let them get to know me, and how to project warmth, and create rapport. Hmmm. That fear could be disastrous for a guy who's trying to help people get into their own businesses!

So I was determined to confront this fear. I made a list of things I could do to beat this fear, including saying hello to as many people as possible and running for public office, which would force me to meet people and let them get to know me.

Thereafter, when I walked into an elevator, I said "hello" to every passenger. At first this was very difficult for me to do. And it was very discomfiting to the passengers! Picture me walking into an elevator in New York City. As I enter, I clap my hands and say, "Hello!" Immediately, everyone steps back to get as far away from me as possible. No one says a word. They're thinking I'm an escapee from a local mental ward. But then I break the ice by saying, "I'm a visitor from Waco, Texas . . . (that's pronounced Wae-co, not whack-o) . . . and I think it's great to be in this city." Now, someone will smile. And if I keep smiling, and looking at them, invariably someone will speak!

Often I've been able to engage people in conversations, even after we've left the elevator. And guess what? I've sold several franchises by meeting people in elevators!

Running for public office to confront fear may sound a bit drastic. It surely wouldn't make a very good campaign theme, and maybe that's why I lost. But it taught me how to meet people, project warmth, and create rapport.

Everyone in town thought I was insane to run for office in the district that I selected. It was a black district that had not had a white candidate for office in the past forty years. The experts predicted that I wouldn't even get 10 percent of the votes. Well, I got 46 percent!

Every Sunday I attended a different church with a black congregation. Fear would never have permitted me to do that before. We prayed together, sang together, and talked together. I asked for their votes. I also went door to door throughout the district. I met many wonderful people, some of whom are still my friends today. And though I wasn't elected, by the time the campaign was over every last vestige of my fear of getting too close to people was gone. And that's one fear that has never stopped me since.

I was never afraid to open my own business and be dependent on myself for an income—even though I'd been raised in a household where we never sat on the living room furniture because we didn't want anything to happen to it! My parents had experienced the Great Depression, and they knew that even if you were all right today, tomorrow you might not be so lucky. Tomorrow you might not have the money to buy new furniture, so you had to be very careful with *everything*.

My first big opportunity to start my own business came when I attended Hofstra University. In class I sat next to a man who was forty years old, had eight children, and lived in an affluent section of Long Island, New York. One day before class I noticed that he was doing paperwork related to his job. I considered him highly successful, and so I asked him what he did for a living.

He told me he worked only four hours every morning at a very simple job: delivering newspapers.

Now wait a minute. When I was ten I had a newspaper route. And while I got good tips, I didn't make enough money to support myself, let alone eight kids.

But this man owned a distributorship. The newspaper carriers worked for him! There was good money in that business, and that's how I got the idea to buy a newspaper distributorship, in spite of my fear of starting my own business and my fear of poverty.

At the time, I didn't know anything about conquering fears. I knew I had fears, but like everyone else, I didn't think about how to master them. Recognizing my fears, however, this man encouraged me. He told me that I could succeed in the same business. As I looked at his paperwork (one of the action steps that would help me conquer my fear), he showed me what the newspaper distribution business was all about. Through many similar meetings he helped build my confidence. And as I grew to believe that I could succeed in my own business, I overcame the fear of getting started.

Once you begin practicing this process, you'll benefit from the domino effect. In the course of mastering one fear, other fears fall apart. As the fears topple, your confidence soars, and eventually, you learn to master your list of fears.

While I was campaigning for public office, I not only got comfortable meeting strangers, I learned how to get closer to people, including members of my family and people at the office. All of my fears related to meeting people, getting to know them, letting them get to know me, and so on disappeared. As a result, I'm a more communicative person, and much more likable. That has bolstered my self-image and helped me face other challenges in my life.

I shudder to think of what I might have become had I not conquered my fear of starting a business. If I had allowed that fear to push me into the box that was already beginning to enclose me, I'd probably still be living in New York today. Like my father, I might have become a good civil servant, happy just to be secure. But, of course, never so secure that my family would have dared to sit on the living room furniture!

I am proof that when you look at your fears, list them in priority, and take action to combat them, you can master them. And in the process you can drive yourself to the peak of success.

Tony Robbins has become well known for teaching people how to overcome their fears. I've attended his seminars and also enrolled my managers in them. The seminars are powerful. After one of them, even the most timid person will walk on a hot bed of coals, barefoot! What's the point? Mastering fears.

I accomplish much the same thing in my seminars, and at graduation ceremonies with my franchisees, by encouraging people to break boards with their bare hands. This is a real test of faith over fear. Most people don't believe they can break a one-inch by twelve-inch board with a bare hand. But in three minutes I've demonstrated how to do it, and they've succeeded.

I tell people to visualize the center of the board, and to think of it as representative of their greatest fear. When they break through the board, they'll break through that fear.

To be successful at breaking a board, you must be focused, you must visualize your fist passing through the board, you must breathe correctly for energy and power, and your team must support you. (Interestingly, these are some of the very same elements that can make you successful in business and life.) I recall one occasion when I asked for a volunteer from my audience to break a board. Usually, there's a pause, followed by nervous laughter, and then some coaxing to get someone to step forward. But this time a very attractive woman with a slight build stepped forward immediately. She was nervous getting up in front of five hundred people, but she couldn't have been as nervous as I was staring at her tiny, slim hand.

I had to remind myself that it's not strength that breaks the board. It's the belief, through focus, visualization, and modeling, that creates the force that will break the board. As I explained to my volunteer, she had to see herself breaking the board, breaking through her fear. Then I broke a board as a demonstration for her to model. When it was her turn, whhhippp, one crack at the board and she broke it easily!

The next volunteer was a man who weighed 240 pounds. I gave him the same instructions I had given the woman before him. He stepped up to the board, stared at the center of it, and hit it hard. His hand bounced off. The board didn't break. He tried it again. The board didn't break. I asked him to check his focus. And I also asked the audience to support him by shouting, "Break the board!" over and over again. This time, he broke the board.

Am I telling you to break boards or walk on coals? Not necessarily. I am telling you to stay focused on your targets—not your fears. That way, you can master your fears with the confidence of people who have participated in these and similar activities.

These activities—like any action that you may take to overcome fears—serve another purpose. They are anchors. They anchor in your mind the experience of conquering a particular fear. Your mind can then trigger the memory of that experience, and you will benefit from the power of that memory.

Nowadays, when I'm confronted with a fear, all I have to do is clench my fist to trigger the memory of when I broke through that barrier, that fear. If I'm in a situation where I'm going to speak to a roomful of strangers, or meet the board of a company that I want to purchase, or deliver a report at a conference, and fear tries to creep into my mind to weaken me, I clench my fist and trigger my first memory of breaking the board. The confidence that I gained during that activity—as drastic as it seemed originally—returns to me, and I'm in control.

Anchoring the process of conquering a fear is important. It will protect you from that fear of life. It was Eleanor Roosevelt who said, "You gain strength, courage and confidence by every experience in which you really stop to look fear in the face. The danger lies in refusing to face the fear, in not daring to come to grips with it. You must make yourself succeed every time. You must do the thing you think you cannot do."

Conquering fear is stimulating. It's a way to get a "rush," an emotional high. Life with control of fear, a mastery of fear, is exciting and fulfilling.

It's impossible to escape fear altogether. In fact, life without fear would be physically dangerous. Fear helps keep us in check. It's damaging, however, when it renders our lives boring and unfulfilling. Conquering fear is stimulating. It's a way to get a "rush," an emotional high. Life with control of fear, a mastery of fear, is exciting and fulfilling.

Target: Worry

What keeps you awake at night? What are you worried about? What terrible things do you think are going to happen?

Ask yourself these questions. Be very clear about what worries you before I tell you some effective ways to stop worrying.

Experts say the human mind can only act on one thought at a time. You can't do your best at something if you're worried that you're going to fail. The mind will focus on your dominant thought of failure, not the subordinate thought of success, and you will fail. Arthur Somers Roche summed up this theory when he wrote, "Worry is a thin stream of fear trickling through the mind. If encouraged, it cuts a channel into which all other thoughts are drained."

Have you ever noticed that once a football player fumbles the ball, he'll often fumble it again during the same game? Either that or he'll become so overly cautious that he won't run well and he won't gain big yardage. Why does that happen? Because he's worrying about fumbling the ball—that's the dominant thought in his mind. And as long as he worries about it, he can't achieve peak performance. Understanding this is a big step toward mastering worry.

"I am an old man and have known a great many troubles, but most of them have never happened," said Mark Twain.

Isn't that the truth? How much time do we waste worrying about things that never happen? And for what purpose? "Worry never robs tomorrow of its sorrow," wrote A.J. Cronin, "it only saps today of its strength."

Consider a scenario that could happen to anyone, and frequently does. You've got an appointment to call on a prospective customer at 9 a.m. tomorrow. This is a "biggie," and you've been waiting for months to get to see this person. Then your lawyer calls and reminds you that you must be in court tomorrow at 9 a.m. or you'll forfeit a case you've been battling for months, a case involving some much-needed money that's owed to you. You got the dates mixed up or you'd never have agreed to meet your prospective customer at 9 a.m. Now what are you going to do? Miss court, and lose the case? Miss your business appointment, and you may never get another one. Either way, you lose.

Is this scenario bad enough to keep you awake tonight?

Here's how I'd solve that problem. I'd do the Worst Possible Outcome Exercise, which involves asking a question over and over again, and answering it. The question: "What is the worst that could happen?"

"What will happen if I cancel the business appointment?" I ask.

"It may rob me of another opportunity to meet with that prospect," I reply.

"What will happen if I don't get another opportunity to meet with that prospect?" I ask.

"I won't sell him. Won't get his business."

"What will happen if I don't get his business?"

"It means I won't make as much money this year."

"What will happen if I don't make as much money this year?"

"Nothing, except that I won't make as much money."

Ah. The worst possible outcome—if I cancel the business appointment—is that I won't make as much money this year. That's not fatal. And it may not even be true, because if I call to cancel the appointment, I might be able to re-schedule it, maybe for later in the day, or the next day.

"What will happen if I don't show up in court?"

"I'll lose the case."

"What will happen if I lose the case?"

"I won't get paid the money that's due me."

"What will happen if I don't get that money?"

"I'll be in trouble. I'll have to borrow money to pay my lawyer. And I'll have a hard time accepting that I lost the case when I should have won it."

The better decision becomes obvious by running through this mental exercise. There's no need to worry about it. You know the worst possible outcome of both options and it's clear that going to court is the better choice.

When I owned a newspaper distribution business, I was under a lot of pressure to get the newspapers delivered on time to the delivery boys and still get myself to school and get my school work done. Occasionally a delivery boy would get sick and leave a note on his door that he couldn't work that day—leaving me with the added task of delivering his papers.

I would sometimes wake up in the middle of the night with knots in my stomach, worried that I would find a note on one of the doors the next morning. One morning, about 3:30, I asked myself, "What's the worst thing that can happen here?" And I figured out that if a route didn't get delivered, I'd lose about $3.00 for that day. Once I analyzed the situation, I slept better, knowing that the worst possible outcome wasn't so bad.

In any worrisome situation, if you gather and analyze the pertinent information and consider the worst possible outcome, it's easy to make a decision without worrying about it. In its simplest terms, worry is nothing but another fear—fear of the unknown. Once you make it known, the fear (worry) goes away. Remember when you were a kid and you thought the monster lived in your closet or under your bed? What did you do? You turned on the lights, you got on your knees and looked under the bed, and you opened the closet door. After that you could stop worrying about a monster getting you during the night. When you could see the situation clearly, there was nothing to worry about.

Earl Nightingale taught the same lesson another way. He told about the two recruits in basic training who were waiting to be shipped out. One was worried sick about going overseas. But his friend said there was no sense worrying about it. As he sized up the situation, he said "There's a fifty-fifty chance you'll be shipped overseas. If you're not, there's nothing to worry about. If you are, there's a fifty-fifty chance you won't see action. If you don't, there's nothing to worry about. If you do, there's a fifty-fifty chance you won't get hurt. If you don't, there's nothing to worry about. If you do, there's a fifty-fifty chance you won't die. If you don't, there's nothing to worry about. If you do, you won't have any more worries. So why worry?"

Lots of people miss the best opportunities of their lives because they worry and procrastinate until it's too late.

Don't worry, be decisive

A lot of people worry about making decisions. Even when they know the worst possible outcome of their options, they still fret about making a decision. And that results in procrastination, which is a time killer and an opportunity buster. Lots of people miss the best opportunities of their lives because they worry and procrastinate until it's too late.

I remember a story that I heard some years ago about a young man in Grand Rapids, Michigan. He had a college internship at the local newspaper, and one of his assignments was to interview a couple of young entrepreneurs who'd started a new business, and write about them. The intern spent the better part of a day with the entrepreneurs, asking lots of questions about how they operated their little cleaning products company. Before he went away, the entrepreneurs offered him the opportunity to join them on the ground floor of their business. Well, he wasn't about to spend his life selling soap! He was a college graduate! What would his friends and family think? He had studied for a career in journalism, after all, not business.

I wonder where that intern is today. I know what happened to the two entrepreneurs, Rich DeVos and Jay Van Andel. Their little soap company is called the Amway Corporation today. DeVos said later, "The only thing that stands between a man and what he wants from life is often merely the will to try it, and the faith to believe that it's possible."

How often have you said, "I could have . . . ." or "I should have . . . ."? You don't ever have to say it again. Program yourself to take action. Don't wait for a better time or a more favorable situation. Make a decision, and do it!

It was Longfellow who wrote, "Whenever two ways lie before us, one easy and the other hard, one which requires no exertion while the other calls for resolution and endurance, happy is the person who chooses the mountain path and scorns the thought of resting in the valley."

As a general rule, people who just can't make up their minds compound problems. Sometimes they say, "I don't want to act hastily . . .there are two sides to every issue." But the reluctance to make up one's mind and act is really based on fear, not judicious thinking. Think about it. If you've got a fear of making decisions, resolve the fear.

I approach decision making like everything else I do, in an orderly fashion. Here are five steps to decision making:

1. Determine the objective, the target.
2. Pull together all the information possible about the situation and consider all your choices.
3. Analyze the obstacles and the opposition.
4. Compare the possible courses of action against each other and consider how each one addresses the obstacles.
5. Make the decision.

Believe me, if you take these steps, your decision is going to be as good, if not better, than that of anyone else who could make the decision for you. No one has a corner on making good decisions. My organization is full of executives, managers, and people at all levels who do not have college educations and who came to work for me with no experience in business, but they make decisions every day. They know how. They learned by making decisions!

And what if you make a bad decision? Well, just ask yourself, "What will happen if . . . ?" until you figure out the worst possible outcome.

Target: Anger

As you may have noticed, the negative emotions are interrelated. You fear something, so you worry about it, and then you're angry. Often, of course, the anger seems to be about something completely unrelated, even trivial. You're worried about making your payroll, so you snap at the child who's making too much noise at home. If you weren't worried about the payroll and fearful of what might happen, you'd probably be playing with your kid, making just as much noise.

Often, anger leads to something worse than yelling at

a child. Husbands beat their wives, wives shoot their husbands, parents abuse their children, lovers kill lovers, children hurt other children. Why? It's anger in action. Often, the people who kill or attack don't even know their victims, but they're still angry. They're angry because they're worried and afraid.

Are you angry with someone? Probably. Everybody seems to be mad at somebody at one time or another. Anger is destructive. It is mentally and physically harmful, as you no doubt know. Anger causes blood pressure to rise, which can result in a stroke or a heart attack. At the very least anger is exhausting. It takes a lot of energy to be mad at someone. And it's just not worth it.

Queen Elizabeth I said, "Anger makes dull men witty, but it keeps them poor." Nothing has changed much since the sixteenth century!

It tickles me to hear how some people deal with anger. "I'll fix that guy!" says the angry wife. "I'm never going to speak to him again." Ha! When someone's really angry, I'd just as soon she didn't talk to me. Angry people talk too *loud*. Of course, the only person who's punished is the person who doesn't talk. She bottles up her emotions, and that can eventually make her sick.

How about the angry people who clench their teeth and say, "I don't get mad . . . I get even." There's a self-defeating attitude. That's merely feeding negative emotion, allowing anger to fuel other, potentially more destructive fires.

I agree with the experts who say that you've got to give someone permission to make you angry. If you do, then it's your fault that you're angry. My decision is not to give people that permission.

But what if you're already angry? Here I go again with the lists. Make a list, right now, of the people you're angry with, and the reasons you allowed them to make you angry.

Name of person with whom I am angry

_____

Reason for my anger

_____

Pick one of the people on your list. Now, rethink the situation that led to your anger. Do you share any of the fault? Okay, let's say you say, "No!" Continue thinking about this person. What are this person's positive qualities? What do you normally like about this person? It might help to record this information on paper. Is there anything about this person that would help you diffuse the anger?

Look, you've got to be practical about people. Anger toward a particular person that can be assuaged only by having that person change will never be assuaged. It will eat you alive! You need to come up with a strategy for interacting with certain people pretty much as they are. Your strategy should help you get the best out of your relationship with that person and ignore the things about him that make you angry.

Remember, people sometimes explode at you not because you did anything but because of fear and worry about events and happenings unrelated to you. (Most people take their anger at themselves out on others.) You were in the wrong place at the wrong time. Suddenly you've given them permission to interfere with your life. In those cases it would be good if you could simply "take it." Help relieve that other person's anger. Say to the person, "You're angry about something, and I don't think it's me. Why don't you tell me what you're angry about?"

If you can't get over your anger with someone, you'd be better off forgetting the situation entirely and never thinking about it, or that person, again.

It's not always practical to wipe a spouse, a child, a parent, or a close friend, out of your mind. You can easily enough forget about certain relatives, neighbors, friends, and business associates. Stay away from them. Don't dwell on the matter that caused your anger. You'll live longer.

But you can't avoid *everyone*. You've got to resolve your anger. Here's what I suggest you do. Go back to the list and start at the top. Telephone each person on the list. Meet them in person if you prefer. But tell each one this: "I'm not angry with you any more. Life's too short." Then, tell them that you think they're a good person, and why. And say no more. You'll feel empowered by this experience, and you'll relieve yourself of some potentially dangerous emotional baggage.

In his book, *Coping With Difficult People*, Dr. Robert Bramson offers five steps for coping with those who make you angry.

1. Assess the situation. Be sure you know why you're angry, and try to figure out what motivated the cause for your anger. What's going on in the other person's life? Why did she say or do whatever it was that made you angry? Was this normal behavior for her? Are you over-reacting to the situation? Will it help if you talk?

2. Stop wishing the person or situation would go away. That won't happen. Frogs turn into handsome princes only in fairy tales.

3. Put some distance between you and the source of your anger. If it's an employee, send her to a seminar for the day, or you attend a seminar. If it's a family member, get away by going to the gymnasium, or to a movie, or out for a walk. You can't fight with people when you're not in contact with them.

4. Make a plan for coping with the person more effectively. Focus on her positive qualities and contributions. Change your interaction with her.

5. Implement your coping strategy. You'll find it's now possible to stay in control.

The best thing to do about anger is not get angry! It's not impossible to do. Why not make it one of your targets?

Target: Guilt

It started while we were still sitting in our high chairs, and it's never ending.

"Eat your peas," your mother said. "You should be happy you've got any food at all because there are children starving in Ethiopia."

What's an American child know about Ethiopia? No matter. The word doesn't register in the child's mind. But the guilt does. The child feels guilty about "having" when others "have not." And in addition, he *hates* peas, forever!

Does the guilt have a long-term effect? Of course it does. It sets in place a guilt-governing limit on how prosperous that person will allow himself to become.

Throughout life we hear phrases like,

"Do you know how hard I worked to clean the kitchen, and now you've messed it up again!" Guilt.

"All I ever asked of you was to get good grades in school, but you couldn't even do that for me." Guilt.

"I've put the best years of my life into this relationship and what has it gotten me?" Guilt.

"But, dad, everyone else's parents can afford it." Guilt.

"The doctor said I should take off a couple of days, but I knew you wanted to be out of the office today, so I came in." Guilt.

Guilt is never-ending. It may be our most common currency. It's also very effective. I wonder what all the psychiatrists and psychologists would do for a living if we eradicated guilt?

This isn't to say that all guilt is bad. How did H.L. Mencken put it? "Conscience is the inner voice that warns us someone may be looking." When our own inner voice assesses our actions and encourages us to contribute back to society in one way or another, that's a constructive and valuable form of guilt. If Albert Schweitzer hadn't felt guilty for having given so little to his fellow man, he'd never have started his mission in Africa. That's good guilt. But guilt laid on by others is destructive and worthless.

Guilt motivates us by making us feel indebted, and sometimes that's bad. A husband wants to strike out on his own as an entrepreneur and he tells his wife his plan. And she says, "I guess I can do without a new kitchen. And since we never go out anyway, I don't need new clothes. Maybe the children can get jobs after school, or on weekends." That's guilt in capital letters. So what's that husband do? He stays in his nice, safe, dead-end, tiny box of a job, where he's full of fear, worry and anger, and he shoves his target dreams to the basement.

Look, you've got to control guilt, or have it control you. Would you let someone choose your food, select your clothes, decide what music you'll listen to, and set up other rules by which you'd be allowed to live? No. But if you allow guilt to control you, that's what you're doing. If you knuckle under because you're afraid you'll hurt someone's feelings or make them unhappy, you're not going to master guilt. But you will master martyrdom! You'll become one of those annoying people who spends time recounting how he sacrificed to appease other people.

So what do you do to master guilt? You don't have to write a list! But here are a couple of techniques that will help you.

Forgive yourself

Do you feel guilty about things from the past? Forgive yourself. If you can take some action to rectify whatever it was you did or didn't do, then set up a plan and take the action. You'll feel better. But if you can't rectify the problem that way, that's okay. Face yourself in the mirror, admit you screwed up royally, forgive yourself once and for all, and move on. Do not confuse making mistakes with being an undeserving person!

At the end of the 1990 football season, Scott Norwood missed the field goal that would have won the Super Bowl for the Buffalo Bills. He should have made that field goal. He had the skill to make it and the opportunity to make it. But he didn't. And the Buffalo Bills went home without their Super Bowl rings.

But when the team arrived in Buffalo, fans were waiting at the airport to cheer and applaud and thank the players, including Scott Norwood. They applauded him for all the field goals he had successfully kicked during their fantastic, winning season. The people of Buffalo proved that making a mistake did not make a bad person, or a bad player.

Everybody screws up. You can't do better by accumulating guilt. You can only do better by learning what there is to learn from the mistake, and then move on with renewed determination to reach all your targets.

Build your self-image

There it is again. One of the characteristics of the successful entrepreneur. Believe in yourself, and build up your own confidence.

Tell the people who regularly pull your strings that you appreciate everything they've done for you, and now you're going to try very hard to make them happy with your new choices. But your life is your life. Not theirs.

Don't waste a minute of it!

Take positive actions

As a business owner, you will frequently be challenged by all four negative emotions: fear, worry, anger, and guilt. I promise you that your success will never be determined by your ability to avoid or escape these emotions; it will be a product of the way you respond to them. When you are immersed in positive, productive actions you free yourself from the negative, destructive results of the Big Four. I'm confident the information in this chapter will help you, if you give it the opportunity.

ACTION ITEM

Your assignment today is to read another book, *The Success System That Never Fails*, by W. Clement Stone. He's the man who's responsible for introducing us to Positive Mental Attitude. His book helped me, and I'm sure you'll learn from it, too. It will help you combat and master the Big Four emotions.

14.
The Power of Influence

"Using fear to influence people doesn't work in the long run."

"Tone of voice is powerful!"

"Have you ever noticed that the people who influence you are usually people you like?"

DON DWYER

What does influence have to do with becoming your own boss, building your own business, achieving target dreams, and seeking happiness in life? I say, *"Everything!"*

So I'm always disappointed when I see someone resist learning the skills needed to be influential. Call it what you will: sales, persuasion, communication, rapport—it's influencing others to see things your way. How good you are at this, quite frankly, determines how successful and happy you'll be as an entrepreneur. People who don't master the power of influence generally end up leading unhappy, unfulfilled, and insecure lives, and frequently they feel unimportant and victimized.

How to influence others

When you start a business, the power of influence is a valuable tool. You'll need to influence bankers, other lenders, equipment vendors, landlords, suppliers, associates, employees, customers, clients, and business neighbors, just to name a few. Entrepreneurs are usually immersed in trying to get others to see things their way.

The ways we influence others are frequently the same ways they influence us. Two of the most common techniques we use are fear and incentives. Let's review these techniques and examine their effectiveness and purpose in our lives.

As explained in the previous chapter, fear is a powerful tool that's capable of holding us in bondage, as well as motivating us to do good things. For example, fear of failure keeps us from starting a business of our own. Fear of heights stops us from participating in certain adventures. Fear of poverty keeps us on our toes at work—otherwise we might get fired. The fear of getting a ticket makes many of us stop at red lights and obey other traffic laws. Fear stops many of us from smoking, lest we have a heart attack and die. In these examples, fear is doing something *to* us, as opposed to our using fear to get our way.

Mastering fear by understanding how it works allows us to use fear productively in our personal lives. On the other hand, some masters of fear use it destructively to influence other people. You probably know the kinds of people I'm talking about. They use their size to intimidate others. They use their strength to intimidate others. They use trickery to incite fear and intimidate others. They get their way using fear or some combination of fears.

If you've ever influenced someone by using a scare tactic, then you know what I'm talking about. But let me ask you: Does influence by fear work? How long does it last? And after you've used this technique, how does it make *you* feel, even if you get your way?

Using fear to influence people is nonproductive for both parties involved. At best, it's usually a temporary solution. Once the fear is removed, the outcome of the influence dissolves. And can anyone really feel good about bullying someone?

Using fear to influence people is of temporary value.

Incentives, or rewards, represent another way to influence people. We first learned about incentives as kids. "Take out the garbage and I'll give you your allowance," parent says to child. I remember when I was ten my parents offered me $1.00 to mow the lawn. At first I was thrilled to do it. But after several weeks went by I found out my friends were getting paid $1.50 and $2.00 to mow similar-sized lawns for their parents. So I complained and asked for more money. My parents refused. When I continued to grumble, they did what any parents would do. They reverted to influence-by-fear and said, "Do it, or else!" I hated mowing the lawn under those conditions!

In businesses where incentives are used to influence people, a similar scenario occurs between employers and employees. Employers who use incentives find that each year the incentives have to get bigger to keep people happy. Until one day the employer realizes, "I'm paying bigger stakes but getting less work!" And that's the end of the incentives. Like fear, incentives have a temporary power; in the long run, they don't work unless attitudinal changes occur.

So how do you influence people in a positive, lasting way? You do it by changing the way *you* think and behave. By doing so, you gain the power of influence over other people. It's an inside-out phenomenon that anyone can learn. In fact, in this book you've learned some of the skills to gain power of influence.

Here are the steps.

- All communication should be based on an honest adherence to your value system. In other words, don't try to influence people to do things that are wrong or bad for them.
- You must learn and practice rapport skills. People who like you will be more easily influenced by you.
- You must build a strong self-image based on your positive attitude. If you're wishy-washy and experience emotional highs and lows, who could be influenced by you?

If you communicate honestly and consistently within your value system, your actions will influence the people you meet and get to know. You won't have to go out of your way to influence people — it will just happen. They will believe what you say because they respect you. They'll find comfort and security in your presence, and unless there are other determining factors you cannot control (ego, ignorance, mental illness, etc.) they will be influenced by what you say.

Target: NLP

In chapter 4 I mentioned Neuro-Linguistic Programming (NLP), a communications discipline now used by millions of people throughout the world. I'm going to draw on some NLP principles to explore the power of influence. But don't be concerned. You don't need to be an NLP expert to learn how to influence others.

You may recall in that earlier chapter my reference to statistics about communications: About 7 percent of our communication is language-based, 38 percent is based on tone of voice, and the remaining 55 percent has to do with physiology or "body language."

This means that *what* you say is not nearly as important as the *way* you say it!

Most people never give much thought to their tone of voice. They just talk, generally allowing their emotions to determine their tone. But radio broadcasters and telemarketers have become very sensitive to the power of tone of voice. Paul Harvey and Walter Cronkite became two of the most trusted men in America because of their tone of voice over the airwaves. And who can forget the influence of Orson Welles when he read The War of the Worlds on radio! The tone of his voice influenced millions of people to panic, although that was not his intention.

Tone of voice is powerful!

Body language or nonverbal communication represents more than half of our communication skills. Facial expressions, hand gestures, posture, even the tiniest physical movements manage to communicate and influence with surprising power. If you're old enough, you'll remember the famous Nixon-Kennedy debate. Those who heard the debate via radio were sure Nixon had won, his tone of voice was so much more influential than Kennedy's. But those who watched the debate on television knew that Kennedy had won. His non-verbal communication was far superior to Nixon's. Body language is powerful!

So to become influential, you must begin by controlling your tone of voice and your body language.

Target: Rapport

Have you ever noticed that the people who influence you are usually people you like? How often have you cast a vote for a politician you didn't like? Few candidates nowadays represent everything we want in a politician, but when it's time to vote, we're going to support the candidate we like best.

People tend to like people who are like them. They listen to people they like, they follow people they like, they vote for people they like, and they are influenced by people they like. NLP teaches that it's possible to *model* another person's tone of voice and body language so that you become *like them*. Modeling helps you build rapport in your relationship with another person. And once you achieve rapport, you're in a powerful position to influence.

Is this dishonest? Modeling someone else, copying someone else, to be like them for the sake of influencing them? Not at all. To some degree, we are like even the people most unlike us. NLP suggests that we downplay how we differ from another person and emphasize how we're alike, especially when we seek to influence that person. If you set out to influence a very quiet, conservative, plodding individual, how effective will you be if you're loud and fast and you don't downplay those characteristics?

I remember one of our franchisees receiving an irate telephone call from a customer. The customer was screaming at her on the telephone. Something had gone wrong and the customer wasn't satisfied with the franchisee's service.

The customer was yelling at the top of his lungs. The franchisee responded calmly, as she would normally do, since she was not a loud or easily excitable person. She spoke quietly to try to "cool off" the customer. It didn't work. Not under those circumstances, anyway. There was no way this customer wanted to hear a quiet, reasonable response.

About then, our franchisee remembered our Power of

Influence training session, which she had attended many months earlier. She started yelling back at the customer. Shouting the same responses that she had already delivered calmly, she got the customer to "cool off"! And the customer said, "I understand your point. I'm sorry I lost my temper. Let's work this out and set up another appointment."

Surprised, the franchisee called me to tell me about her experience. As we say in our training, giving people a reflection of themselves, even exaggerating the reflection a bit, will force them to modify their behavior. In this case, my franchisee was able to alter the unhappy customer's behavior for the better by mirroring the customer's actions.

Mirroring the other person's physical appearance is a powerful influencing method. If the person leans forward and becomes more intense, do the same. If the person sits back and crosses one leg over another, do the same. You'll be amazed at the feeling, the sense of rapport that quickly develops.

Modeling, or mirroring, is an incredibly powerful influencing technique. Apply it to both tone of voice and body of language. If the person across the negotiating table from you leans forward and looks more intense, do the same. If the person eases back and crosses one leg over another, do the same. You'll be amazed at the feeling, the sense of rapport that quickly develops.

You can communicate with your body language, too. If you hunch your shoulders, you convey depression or inferiority. Push your shoulders back, keep your posture straight, and you convey optimism and confidence. You can even change your state of mind by changing your body language. What's more, you'll influence others' opinions about you when you alter your physiology positively.

Let's say you're going to the bank for a loan to start your business. No guarantees (you already know what I think about the American banking system), but these methods of influence *will* improve your chances of getting a loan.

- Dress like your banker. That's not hard to do in the majority of cases. Bankers are conservative people. Male bankers wear white shirts, suits, ties, and wing-tip shoes. Female bankers wear suits, sometimes with flashy accents such as scarves or jewelry. Check out your banker's dress style before you go for your loan request, and dress accordingly.

- Use confident, optimistic body language when you meet the banker. Smile. Offer your hand for a firm handshake. Carry a briefcase and have your papers neatly organized inside.

- Once your banker begins to speak, monitor her tone of voice, the speed at which she speaks, and her inflections. Then model the banker's speech. Talk like your banker.

- Watch the banker's body movements. Gently copy some of them as you continue to converse.

- Emphasize the qualities and tendencies in yourself that appear to match your banker's; suppress the qualities and tendencies that appear not to fit.

As you apply these modeling techniques, you'll build rapport with your banker, and you will have an easier time getting her to agree with your points of view and, ultimately, to grant you a loan.

Monkey see—monkey doesn't

I've always liked that old saying, "Monkey see, monkey do," and it appears to work for animals and children but not so well for adults. That's because some people see (they're visual), some people hear (they're auditory), and some people feel (they're kinesthetic). Most people are dominated by only one of these three orientations. So an auditory person isn't easily influenced by a visual person, or a kinesthetic person, and so on.

Think of this analogy. If you want to communicate with someone by telephone, it will only work if you both speak on the same phone line! If you want to influence a visual person, you've got to be on the visual phone line. An auditory person? Get on the auditory phone line. A kinesthetic person? Get on the kinesthetic phone line.

What if the visual phone line is your favorite—the one you like to use? And you want to influence an auditory person? Or you're kinesthetic and you want to influence a visual person? Very simple. Change your behavior to model the other person. Get on the other person's phone line!

The trick is to figure out whether the person across the table from you is visual, auditory, or kinesthetic. The sooner you know, the faster you'll communicate, and the easier it will be to influence that person.

Visual people

People who use phrases like, "I see it this way," or "I get the picture" are visual people. They would enjoy Ralph Waldo Emerson's message, "Go often to the house of thy friend, for weeds choke the unused path." They see things clearly. They've got minds like blackboards. Sometimes, you can't erase the information they see on their blackboards. Visual people also typically talk and walk quickly, and they breathe high in their chests.

Auditory people

People who say, "That's what I'm hearing," or "It sounds good to me," are auditory people. They would appreciate George Eliot's message, "I like not only to be loved, but to be told that I am loved; the realm of silence is large enough beyond the grave." Usually, auditory people talk in the mid-range tone, and at a medium tempo. They breathe from the center of their bodies and move at a moderate pace.

Kinesthetic people

The touchy-feely people are kinesthetic. They talk low and slow. They love to touch and hug. What you say to kinesthetic people is overpowered by your body language. Handshakes are important to them. And even when it's not spontaneous, a hug or a hearty pat on the back will make them warm up to you.

I know a football coach who understands and uses these techniques, and I love to watch him interact with his players during a game. One night, one of his players made a great tackle. When that player came to the sidelines, I watched the coach stand very close to him and talk into his ear for several minutes with great intensity. A few minutes later, another player caught a long pass for a big gain of yardage. As he came to the sideline, the coach grabbed him, hugged him, whacked him on the helmet, and slapped him on the buttocks. But he hardly said a word to him. This coach knew each of his players, and he knew how to influence them individually.

You may have experienced the clash of visual, auditory, kinesthetic orientations the first time you fell in love. When we first meet someone we really like and hope to get to know better, we automatically use all three influencing methods to build the relationship. But as time passes, and we get more comfortable with one another, we tend to use our dominate orientation. The problem occurs when our orientation isn't the same as our partner's.

One of my sons had a beautiful girlfriend who was visual. She wanted him to *look* at her, to notice the changes she made (frequently) to her hair, make-up, and clothing. She wanted to be visually appreciated. But my son is kinesthetic. He wanted to hold hands with her, hug her, kiss her, and in that way show her how much he cared for her. When they were together, she wanted to be looked at and he wanted to touch. Well, that relationship didn't last long. I know what I would have told him to do. If he had looked at her and recognized her beauty, *plus* touched her, they might have lasted.

Once you begin to use these techniques, you will achieve the Power of Influence.

ACTION ITEM

If the subject matter of this chapter has piqued your curiosity and you want to know more about the techniques that can help you become more influential, I recommend that you read *Unlimited Power* by Tony Robbins, and *Non-verbal Communication* by Ken Cooper.

But more importantly, start practicing the techniques today. Begin with yourself. Figure out whether you're a visual, auditory, or kinesthetic person. Examine your spouse, your children, your boss, and your business associates. Begin to respond to them in their dominant orientations, and just watch your influencing powers improve.

15.
Mental Aerobics

"You can build the business of your dreams, if you just begin to see yourself in that business!"

"If I talked to you the way you talk to you, you would never talk to me again!"

"Be positive!"

DON DWYER

No doubt you'd agree that genuinely confident people are more influential, successful, and happier than people who lack confidence. So the question seems to be, "How do I become a genuinely confident person?"

Mental aerobics will help. They are the techniques of self-talk, visualization, and positive thinking. Mental aerobics will help you create a state of mind in which you gain immediate powers. Here's how it works.

Close your eyes and think of a time in your life when you felt absolutely loved. Think of a specific time. What happened to you to make you feel that way? Was it something that was said? Was it a certain look? How did it feel? And what did you say to yourself, and to others, when you experienced this feeling?

Now think of a time when you were totally happy.

Think of a specific time. (If you've never been totally happy, imagine what it would be like). What happened to make you feel so happy? Then, combine the feelings of happiness and love, and hold them in your mind.

Next, think of everything you have to be thankful for. Your loved ones, your health, the great country you live in, the opportunities you enjoy. And then, combine these feelings of thankfulness with your feelings of happiness and love.

Finally, remember a time in your life when you were powerful. Think of a specific time. What happened? What did you do? Or what did others say to you to make you feel so powerful? How did you visualize yourself? Relive this moment of success. And then combine these feelings with your feelings of thankfulness, happiness, and love.

Sit quietly for fifteen seconds. Then, clap your hands, open your eyes, and experience what you feel. Are you relaxed? Do you feel you're in control? Do you feel happy, loved, thankful, and powerful? I bet you do.

In just a few minutes' time, you created for yourself a state of mind that gave you tremendous powers. Practice these mind aerobics often throughout the day, and you'll acquire genuine confidence.

Target: Self-talk

Begin feeling confident about yourself by believing your own story. If you're a business person, be in a business that makes you proud, one that provides quality goods and valuable services and gives your customers their money's worth. Conduct your business responsibly and positive results will follow. That makes it easier to believe in yourself.

The way you communicate with yourself determines how you'll communicate with others. Think of this: If I talked to you the way you talk to you, you would never talk to me again!

For example, say you drop something and break it. "You clumsy idiot, you did it again!" you say to yourself. If a friend spoke to you that way, you might never talk to him again. So why is it OK for you to do it to yourself? Every time you use negative self-talk, you tear down your all-important self-image.

What you say to yourself, about yourself, accumulates

below the conscious level of your mind and exerts significant control over your present and future thoughts and behaviors. What you communicate to yourself via body language does the same thing. Would you rather say and do positive things, or negative things?

Negative self-talk, and negative target visualization (picturing negative images of yourself) is what keeps alcoholics drinking, smokers smoking, gamblers gambling, and overweight people overeating. The fortunate people who have tried self-talk techniques know what tremendous benefits they can deliver when used positively.

Catch yourself in the act of doing something right, and praise yourself for it. Make a point to stop every time you act "successfully" and tell yourself, "That was a good job!"

In his book, *The One Minute Manager*, Ken Blanchard advises bosses to catch people in the act of doing something right and praise them for it. You ought to follow the same advice for yourself. Catch yourself in the act of doing something right and praise yourself for it. Make a point of stopping every time you act "successfully" and tell yourself, "That was a good job!"

I'm talking about little things: finding your way to an office you've never visited before without wasting any time; handling a telephone call especially well; telling an eloquent, funny joke; holding back a temper outburst or handling a sensitive matter; and so on. Give yourself some mental applause for each of these accomplished tasks.

It would be better, by the way, not to talk to yourself at all than to talk to yourself negatively. Consider the story of two amateur runners, Harry Botkins and Jim Collins. They were about the same age and the same build and they shared the same dream: to finish among the top two hundred in a marathon race that attracted at least a thousand competitors.

Interestingly, Botkins and Collins also had the same faulty running stride. So a couple of months before the marathon, the runners attended a clinic where they were videotaped in action. A coach, pointing to their weakness, told them how to correct the problem. And now, the similarities of the story end.

Botkins and Collins used the information in different ways, and with opposite results. Botkins cursed himself under his breath for "running like a duck," and swore to improve his stride if it killed him. Collins, on the other hand, didn't get upset. He was pleased to have the new information and eager to apply it so that he would run better, faster.

Instead of thinking about the problem, Collins concentrated on the corrective moves. Before each practice run thereafter, he spent a few moments visualizing how he would run correctly using the efficient stride the coach had demonstrated for him. And as he ran, he also kept the picture of the perfect stride in his mind. By doing so, Collins emphasized the positive and eliminated the negative, first mentally, then physically.

At first, Collins' running time got worse! But he wasn't discouraged. He told himself that he was reconditioning his body and his mind to propel him forward using the new techniques. Although his stride made him feel uncomfortable, he told himself that he needed time to learn how to use his muscles differently.

After three weeks of positive self-talk, positive visualization, and practice, Collins was running faster than ever. Every day, as he got closer to the marathon date, he felt stronger. And on the day of the marathon, when the starter's pistol was fired, Collins ran the best race of his life.

Now what happened to the negative thinker, Botkins? After the clinic, he also continued to practice, but every day he reminded himself, "Don't run like a duck." Yet no matter how hard he tried, he continued to run like a duck. After two weeks, he realized he wasn't getting any better. And then he began to sustain minor injuries. His ankle bothered him after every workout. Then he pulled a muscle and he couldn't practice for a week.

By the time Botkins returned to his practice runs, he felt defeated. The pain in his ankle was so severe that he had to quit running for a couple of weeks. Gradually he started running again, but by the time of the marathon he was worried about his injuries, and now all he wanted to do was finish the race. When the starter's pistol sounded,

Botkins ran hard, telling himself, "Don't run like a duck, you idiot."

During the race, you can imagine what happened. Collins, the positive self-talker, continued to remind himself how he looked when he ran correctly. And he finished stronger than ever before, coming in eighty-eighth. As he cooled down beyond the finish line, he congratulated himself, and then he set a target for next year: to finish in the top fifty!

I'd put my money on Collins achieving any target he set his mind to!

Then there was Botkins. Poor Harry. His ankle pained him so severely that he had to quit three miles from the finish line. He was bitter, and he told himself, "That's what you get for running like a duck. I guess my running days are over."

Collins and Botkins are good examples of how self-talk and visualization can work for or against you. Keep the wrong things in your mind and you'll perform poorly at whatever you try to do. But keep positive things in mind and you'll reach your targets.

We all use self-talk, even if we're not conscious of it. We don't always say the words out loud. But we talk to ourselves through every decision we make. If you want to take control of your life, don't let your self-talk be negative. Speak to yourself positively.

For instance, if you want to be successful, your self affirmations might sound something like this: "I am successful. I lead people. I run my own company. I earn the trust of others. I attract wealth. I am rich and successful. I win."

The list can be as long or as short as you desire. But the sentences should be simple and always stated positively. Never use a negative verb. Always construct the affirmations so that they direct you toward your targets. Make your affirmations specific and personal.

Many successful people who have used self-talk effectively tape their affirmations to the mirror they look at in the mornings and at night. That way, they're reminded to say their affirmations aloud several times a day. It's a great idea.

The more often you use self-talk techniques, the faster you'll benefit. Your attitude will change dramatically.

Eventually you will become, or you will represent, the person you describe in your affirmations. And as you grow to believe your own story, your affirmations will be reflected in the eyes of other people, including the people you want to influence.

My system for self-talk is to create a Self-Talk Data Bank. This is a collection of ideas, words of wisdom, and encouragement that are important to me. I keep my Self-Talk Data Bank on index cards, although you could also use a file system or a three-ring binder. My Self-Talk Data Bank has helped me change certain attitudes in my life, including achieving targets.

For example, there was a time in my life when I really didn't like people. I didn't enjoy being around them. I was my own worst enemy. And I eventually realized this was an attitude that I would have to change, particularly if I was going to succeed in the franchise business. So I started telling myself, as often as I could remember, "I like people." I looked for good things about every person I met, so I could tell myself, "I like that person because . . . ." For a double punch, I'd say to myself, "People are God's greatest miracles." I collected the positive thoughts in my Self-Talk Data Bank to remind me to repeat them again and again. At first, my old self-talk was fighting for recognition, telling me I didn't like people. That sort of war goes on in our minds all the time, especially when we're trying to change an attitude. However, through repetition, I won, and it works that way every time.

If you use this process and make it a habit, I guarantee it will work. "What's going on in the inside shows on the outside. Whatever we plan in our other-than-conscious mind and nourish with repetition and emotion will one day become a reality," said Earl Nightingale. And psychologist David Viscott agrees: "You must begin to think of yourself as becoming the person you want to be." By the way, your Self-Talk Data Bank can have as many different departments as you want. It's up to you to choose the areas of your life that need to be improved and changed. Use it well, and your Self-Talk Data Bank will become one of your most important possessions.

The combination of mind and emotion in the exercise of visualization is the driving force that will help you reach your target.

Target: Visualization

Positive visualization is the process of creating a precise mental picture of the target you want to achieve. The combination of mind and emotion in the exercise of visualization is the driving force that will help you reach your target.

Like self-talk, visualization affects your attitude and your position in life. If you make your mental image clear enough, picture it strongly enough in your mind, and believe in it firmly enough, repeatedly, then the infinite power of the mind will rapidly make your mental image a reality. On the other hand, I think it's obvious that people who lose are negative visualizers.

Experts tell us that the subconscious mind cannot tell the difference between what actually happened and what we imagined happened. This means we can enjoy a target long before we reach it. It also suggests that you should begin to see things as they will be, not as they are. Imagine what you want most from life, and then picture your existence as if you already achieved your dreams.

Charles Garfield, who has made a lifelong study of top achievers, discovered that most peak performers use mental rehearsal or visualization skills before an important contest. These successful men and women mentally run through every element of important events before they occur. That way, they're ready for the contest. They've already won in their minds, before the race begins.

The Olympic diver Greg Louganis explained his gold-medal performance by saying he visualized every move of the dive. He saw himself walk to the end of the diving board, position his body, jump into the air, and then he watched his body form a straight line as he entered the water cleanly, like a knife through butter. Even though he'd hit his head on an earlier dive, his intense visualization training kept him on course for the real win.

Maxwell Maltz, the plastic surgeon who developed Psychocybernetics, advised people to "Study the situation thoroughly, go over in your imagination the various courses of action possible to you, and the consequences which can and may follow from each course. Pick out the course which gives the most promise—and go ahead."

Today, visualization techniques are being used by performers to conquer stage fright. A study of ninety-four musicians was conducted by Dr. Duncan Clark, a psychiatrist at the University of Pittsburgh, and Dr. Stewart Agras, a psychiatrist at Stanford University. Their findings were reported in the American Journal of Psychiatry in 1991. They discovered that performers who were paralyzed by stage fright responded better to visualization therapy than to drugs. Experiencing their performance by simulation was superior to any other method of controlling their fears.

All of this is to suggest that we can overcome any obstacle if we just harness the power of our other-than-conscious mind. This information ought to excite you if you're planning to become an entrepreneur. It says that you can build the business of your dreams if you just begin to see yourself in that business!

The proof is that others have already done it. Conrad Hilton, as a boy, pictured himself owning a large chain of hotels. His business career developed just as he planned it. Kemmons Wilson, the founder of Holiday Inns, told his wife that he would build four hundred hotels before he built even one. He went on to build thousands before he resigned from Holiday Inns. The hair stylist Vidal Sassoon visualized a life creating new hair styles. He imagined what his salons would look like and where they'd be located, and he achieved it all while still a young apprentice in London.

As for me, I was only a boy when I first visualized myself owning a large, profitable business. I knew I would help provide opportunities to build America, and I saw how I'd do it. As a child I couldn't say exactly how my dream would be fulfilled, or in what form of business it would occur, but I planned my success well in advance. As the old saying goes, "Plan your work, and work your plan." If you do, dreams will come true!

There are two effective ways to implement visualization in your life.

The visualization board

Hang a bulletin board in your bedroom where you can see it first thing in the morning and last thing at night. You can hang it inside your closet door to keep it out of the way and to keep it private. This is your personal dream board.

On the Visualization Board, pin up pictures of all your tangible targets. These might include luxury sports cars, boats, a summer home, vacations, a building with your name on it, or whatever else is important to you.

Also include pictures of people who represent qualities that you want to develop. They may be pictures of famous people, people you've never met, historic figures, or friends, or relatives.

Every morning, look at your Visualization Board. Spend time—as much time as possible—meditating about the person you will become, how you will look, how you will feel, and the targets you will have achieved. Repeat this exercise before you go to bed at night.

You can increase the effect of your Visualization Board by reading books about people who have achieved any or all of your goals. Read biographies of people you admire. Picture yourself interacting with these people, learning from them, modeling them.

Things remembered

This exercise requires that you concentrate on the objects in a room of your choice. Then go to another room and list what you saw in the first room. When you're finished, return to the first room and check your list. Make another list of all the contents you missed. If you've never done this before, you'll be surprised at how many things you miss.

I use this exercise in many different situations. It's a great use of time when I'm waiting in a store, reception room, or airport. By practicing this exercise, you'll improve your concentration and recall.

You can use the skills of this exercise to help you focus on seeing the future exactly the way you want it to be. You want a new house? Picture it clearly. See yourself walking up to the front door and placing your key in the lock. See your furnishings inside. Visualize each room, with all its contents. See your spouse and children waiting for you. Imagine the sounds of the house. The smell of the house. Make it as real to you today as it will be in the future, when your visualized target becomes a reality.

The mind is like a camera. If it's out of focus, our targets will be out of focus. How can you hit what you can't see? But visualization will put your mind in focus.

The mind is like a camera. If it's out of focus, our targets will be out of focus. How can you hit what you can't see? But visualization will put your mind in focus. It will help you achieve targets, build your self-image, and gain genuine confidence.

Target: Positive thinking
I hope you're not one of those people who makes fun of positive thinking. Many people do, you know. And they are usually unsuccessful people.

Through my franchise business, I've been able to associate with some of the most successful people in the world. They've included entrepreneurs, financiers, public speakers, authors, and consultants. I have yet to meet and talk with an exceptionally successful person, in any field, who wasn't a devotee of positive thinking. Not one!

On the other hand, I've listened to any number of people make fun of positive thinking, talk about it sarcastically, and accuse its believers of being simple-minded. And those people always seem to be folks who haven't accomplished much success, let alone self-confidence.

One thing I try to instill in our franchise owners is "Be Positive!"

I start every day by saying, "This is the happiest day of my life." I expect wonderful things to happen to me *every day*. And I'm never surprised that they do! Today is truly the only day we have. Yesterday is a canceled check, a receipt for something done and gone. Tomorrow is a promissory note we don't know whether we'll be able to redeem. But today is here, it's like cash in our hands. We can either make it pay off, or we can squander it.

Now there are two ways you can respond to my philosophy.

You can say I'm a Pollyanna, a fool who is out of touch with reality. And criticize me, and my book, for being simplistic.

Or, you can give my approach a try.

I tell you this: Your success will be in direct proportion to the positive actions you take today and every day. These actions will result in both victory and defeat. Both will make you a better, stronger person, if you accept them in a positive frame of mind. General Douglas MacArthur wrote, "Build me a son, oh Lord, to be humble and gentle in victory, and proud and unbending in defeat."

Those words have given me the courage to handle my defeats while realizing that without the help of others, I would experience no victories.

It's been my experience that people who practice positive self-talk and positive visualization, and who keep a positive attitude, get more accomplished, have more fun in life, attract more successful people, and influence others more often and more easily than people who do not. And oh yes, they are the genuinely confident people.

ACTION ITEM

Dr. Norman Vincent Peale, the beloved author of numerous books about positive thinking, once asked: "What would you do if you knew you could not fail?" It's a stimulating question. I'd answer, "I'd do exactly what I'm doing now." But how would *you* answer Dr. Peale's question? Reflect on his question now, and answer it. Then turn your answer into targets that you can begin to visualize. Imagine that your answer is already reality. Talk to yourself as though you were already living your answer. Think positively about it, and expect it to become true.

16.
The Power of Leadership

"How do you become an enabler?"

"Leaders give to get!"

"Through my years of experience, I've learned to avoid the losers and pick the winners."

"Would you hire yourself? Why?"

DON DWYER

For many years, early in my business career, I was a loner. I considered myself a recluse; I was introverted and fiercely independent. I thought I would be happiest running a one-man shop.

I had been succeeding alone for quite some time when I joined Success Motivation Institute (SMI), where I was introduced to an entirely different philosophy. Paul J. Meyer, the guiding force at SMI and one of the world's leading motivators, was always preaching the importance of recruiting good people, training them well, supporting them effectively, and using this process to multiply your own efforts and abilities. Thanks to Meyer's influence, I decided to give up my Lone Ranger attitude and learn to multiply my opportunities and earnings.

To do so, I had to become a leader. I needed the power of leadership.

At SMI I started recruiting and training distributors to make good presentations and to sell successfully. Although this was difficult at first, the payoff was quickly evident, and the profits motivated me to keep at it. I also discovered an added benefit: the emotional high that I derived from helping others discover their hidden abilities, expand their vision, establish new targets, and achieve greater success and happiness. Wow! That was enormously satisfying.

Looking back, I realize that I acquired leadership skills, and they in turn helped me succeed at recruiting my own army of entrepreneurs, not only at SMI but later in my own organization. Those skills helped land my photograph on the cover of Entrepreneur magazine in 1985 as the leader of one of the fastest-growing franchise companies in the world, and it has helped my company retain its number-one industry status in the same magazine for five years! Plus it has brought my story to the attention of *Success* magazine, the *Wall Street Journal*, *USA Today*, and many other publications.

I've become fascinated by trying to make leadership work as a win-win situation; a win for me, a win for the other person.

The future growth and expansion of my company depends on convincing more and more quality people to join our team. And one of the qualities these people seek is leadership. Today I believe people would agree that I've become a competent leader. I've certainly developed a profound appreciation for the power of leadership. I've become fascinated by trying to make leadership work as a win-win situation; a win for me, a win for the other person (employee, business associate, franchisee, friend, neighbor, etc.).

If you're going to build a business, you'll need the

power of leadership. Perhaps my own experiences will help you develop that power.

The payoff for the ethical person is a reputation for honesty. It's a payoff that makes every undertaking easier and attracts unsolicited opportunities. It's also a payoff that results in strong friendships based on trust. And I don't think there's anything more rewarding.

Target: Ethics

Don't think I changed subjects on you by introducing ethics. Ethics is one of the basic qualities of a leader. The word means doing things morally, obeying laws, knowing right from wrong, and choosing right. The payoff for the ethical person is a reputation for honesty. It's a payoff that makes every undertaking easier and attracts unsolicited opportunities. It's also a payoff that results in strong friendships based on trust. And I don't think there's anything more rewarding.

I spent some of my early life in Brooklyn, a tough borough of New York City, where the prevailing Golden Rule said—and still may—"Do unto them *before* they do unto you." A challenging environment for the ethical person, wouldn't you agree?

I never liked the law-of-the-jungle attitude. I much prefer a business environment based on trust. Perhaps I got that idea by watching a lot of westerns, where a man's word was his bond. Cowboys didn't need contracts drawn up by costly lawyers. A simple handshake committed a man to any venture. Sure made it easy to do business, given those standards.

Now I live in Texas, a long way from Brooklyn in more than just distance. It's also light years away in philosophy. Here you can usually count on what people commit to you. Here the handshake agreement still works. This way of life dates back to the frontier days. It's an environment of self-reliance, but it builds friendships that last for decades. Here in the West the way of life a century ago seems closer than it did back East. In Texas we still seem to know what it means to depend on each other for survival.

Of course, Texas isn't the only state with ethics. No

matter where you are, ethical people create the environments that produce leaders.

Ethics also builds self-image, and we all know by now that self-image is a key to wealth. Anything that diminishes our self-image diminishes our earning power. Ethical people tend to like themselves. They think well of themselves because they do the right things, not necessarily every time, but most times. And those are the kinds of people who have the power to lead.

Napoleon Hill said, "We are constantly punishing ourselves for every wrong we commit and rewarding ourselves for every act of constructive conduct in which we indulge." The ethical person finds more reasons to reward than to punish. Consequently, the ethical person is better prepared to lead.

Absolutely nothing you say, no rules you lay down, will ever influence your people more than your behavior. What you do is more important than what you say. And ethics is all about doing.

If you are the leader of a company, when you hire employees, they will automatically look to you as a role model. Absolutely nothing you say, no rules you lay down, will ever influence your people more than your behavior. What you do is more important than what you say. And ethics is all about doing.

Target: Pick winners
Leaders like winners. Winners are drawn to leaders. Quite a few losers are drawn to leaders, too, however, if for no other reason than they're looking for someone to carry them through life. Through my years of experience, I've learned to avoid the losers and pick the winners.

My strategies for picking winners are based on common sense. Still, since they have helped me select outstanding employees and franchisees, they may prove valuable to you as you build your business and your team of personnel or business associates. Here are some tips.

Look for desire

Perhaps you'll recall my treatment of desire in chapter 3. So you won't be surprised that the first quality I look for when I select an employee, or a franchisee, is passionate desire.

Once upon a time, when I needed to hire someone for my newspaper distribution business, I would drop by the playground and ask a group of kids if they were interested in earning extra money. Everybody was, of course! Until they found out what was involved—especially getting up early in the morning, in all weather conditions! Then I'd lose most of the group.

The kids' questions usually identified which ones had desire. It was fairly easy to tell the winners from the losers. For example, the boys I wouldn't hire would ask these questions:

"How many hours do I have to work?"

"How heavy a load do I have to carry?"

"How far do I have to go?"

"Do I have to work if it's raining (snowing)?"

Less often, I'd hear these questions, which only winners asked:

"How much money can I make?"

"When can I get started?"

"Will you teach me what to do?"

The winners had the desire, obviously. And by recruiting them and leading them, I was able to build the largest circulation distribution business in the history of the *York Daily News*. With a force of two hundred deliverers, we signed up more than ten thousand homes! Desire happen. And ever since, I've looked for desire.

Look for matching values

The second strategy I use in selecting my team is to find out whether their values ues and the values of my organization. For this is a big indicator, not to be minimi

Look for adversity

Finally, I pay special attention

adversity and weathered the storm. I feel sorry for people who were born with silver spoons in their mouths. They don't know about the satisfaction that you gain from working your way up from the bottom, pulling yourself out of poverty or debt. People who have been down, and got up, have had the best education of all.

Many of our top franchisees—I'm talking about people who have become quite wealthy—were once stuck in dead-end jobs, or grew up in poverty, or they had awful financial problems for any number of reasons. I identify with these people. I find it easier and especially rewarding to get them started in a new, positive, lucrative life. I know that if they work with me, their chances of failing are very slim, as long as they're willing to follow my guidelines.

Recently, an increasing number of our franchisees are coming from middle-management and other white-collar jobs, where corporate downsizing is introducing adversity to millions of people. As a means of making good on their adversity, many of these people are seeking opportunities that combine personal and financial growth. They're looking to replace job security (which was a false security) with businesses of their own.

These three strategies—my search for desire, matching values, and adversity—determine who I want to join ~m. And they've been very effective evaluators.

~ by giving more

That makes sense, doesn't it? But it's
~ be a one-man band in a room
~ the growth of your organi-
~ies among the play-

must give up
~ used to do, by
~ing responsibili-
~lized in your own
~anization that way.
~am—will not have an
~ you or your business.
~ity, then you're learning
~e amazing things happen,
~heir skills, their confid~

and their self-images—and your business exceeds your own expectations.

I'm very fortunate to have employees, business associates, and franchisees who would do just about anything for me. A reporter interviewed one of my employees, Jesse Franklin, and was shocked to hear him say, "If Don Dwyer called me tonight and said, 'We're marching into hell at 6 a.m.,' I'd show up at 5 a.m.!" The reporter wondered if I hadn't organized my own cult.

No, I've simply become an enabler. I'm not charismatic, and I'm not a hypnotic wizard. But I have created an environment that enables people to grow personally and financially, and for that, my employees, business associates, and franchisees have allowed me to become their leader.

How do you become an enabler? Here's my formula. It says it all for anyone who wants to acquire the power of leadership.

- Lead by example.
- Recruit people with desire and matching values who have survived adversity.
- Invest in the education and training of your people.
- Teach people to make good decisions; support them when they make mistakes.
- Delegate authority.
- Praise.
- Allow people to make mistakes.
- Believe that people can do more than they think they can do—make them stretch.
- Communicate, using all possible communications skills.
- Build a team: together everyone achieves more.
- Project what you expect. Set targets for your organization and your people.
- Inspect what you expect.

THE HEW THEORY

Honesty Equals Wealth—the HEW Theory—offers many people a compelling reason to be honest with themselves and others.

Many people are honest because of their religious upbringing. They are taught that damnation follows dishonesty, or that God will be pleased if they are honest.

Yet many people, including religious people, are occasionally dishonest. Some more than occasionally.

If you understand the HEW Theory, however, you realize that dishonesty lowers your self-esteem—and in turn inhibits your ability to earn the wealth you desire and deserve.

The HEW Theory makes it easy to do what's right. It's simply another mental tool that can help you reach your potential.

ACTION ITEM

Take some time to think of people who have demonstrated leadership qualities to you. Who are the leaders you know? Make a list of them today. The list could include your boss, coworkers, spouse or relatives, and friends, as well as historical figures, people you've met through books, television, or other media. It makes no difference how long you make your list.

Now, why do you consider the people on your list leaders? What did they do to deserve that honor? List their qualities. Explain your reasoning.

To become a leader, you'll need to develop the same or similar qualities. Would you say you're already on track? How can you speed up that process? And if you're not on track, how can you get there?

Use your answers to set some targets for your life, and then proceed to achieve those targets.

17.
Success—Today

"Do you want to be successful?"

"I hear an inner voice that speaks to me constantly, keeping me on course, guiding me toward the completion of my mission, a lifetime of work."

DON DWYER

Throughout the chapters of this book I've asked you a lot of questions that I hope have been fruitful ones for you. These are the questions and answers that ultimately lead to a successful, happy entrepreneurial life.

By now I hope you realize that you can get more of what you want out of life, including success in business, by asking yourself better questions. Dr. Edward Kramer, inventor of the famous Thank-U-Gram, said, "Man is blind until he achieves insight, and deaf until he hears his own inner voice." Those are the benefits of asking yourself better questions and answering them honestly.

And so, as you might guess, I've got another question or three for you in this final chapter.

Do you want to be successful?

That's a no-brainer. "Yes," says everyone. "Who doesn't want to be successful?"

Okay, but let me ask you a more difficult question.

What's your definition of success?

When I present this question to seminar audiences, I've usually got to press to get an answer. When I do, there are two common answers: Money and Happiness. Few people can get clearer or more specific than those two words.

If you're going to be successful in business, or in life, you must be able to define success clearly so that you'll recognize it when you achieve it.

I encourage you to look behind the symbolic words we commonly use to define success. Otherwise you may never know your real feelings about the meaning of success. If you're going to be successful in business, or in life, you must be able to define success clearly so that you'll recognize it when you achieve it.

An anonymous poet left us with this thought: "Before God's footstool to confess, A poor soul knelt and bowed his head; 'I failed,' he wailed; The Master said, 'Thou didst thy best—that is success.'"

Booker T. Washington said, "Success is to be measured not so much by the position that one has reached in life as by the obstacles which he has overcome while trying to succeed."

I especially like Robert Louis Stevenson's definition (with a couple modern-day, parenthetical alterations): "That man (or woman) is a success who has lived well, laughed often and loved much; who has gained the respect of intelligent men (and women) and the love of children; who has filled his niche and accomplished his task; who leaves the world better than he found it, whether by an improved poppy, a perfect poem or a rescued soul; who never lacked appreciation of earth's beauty or failed to express it; who looked for the best in others and gave the best he had."

Your definition of success should be so clear that you never lose sight of it. It becomes the most important target in your life, and you're constantly aiming for it, trying again and again until you hit the bullseye.

To define success, I suggest that you begin with generalities and then become more specific. It doesn't matter, however, specifically how you approach the definition. It's just important that you define success in your own terms.

To define success in general terms is to speak broadly of your attitudes about success. You're now talking about the "big picture," explaining your basic attitudes about success in life and success in business. Nothing in your general definition of success should depend on other people or events, although it would not be unusual for your general definition to be the same or similar to the definitions of many other people.

For example, many people would be able to relate to my three general definitions of success, which are as follows.

Success without integrity is fleeting and empty. Success compatible with ethical values is lasting and meaningful. We must constantly work to achieve the targets that will validate our value systems, leading to success.

First, *success is the continuing advancement towards value-based targets*. By this I mean that success has a moral and ethical quality based on a person's value system. Success without integrity is fleeting and empty. Success compatible with ethical values is lasting and meaningful. We must constantly work to achieve the targets that will validate our value systems, leading to success. It's an old cliché, but I think it's true: Success is a journey, not a destination.

Without passion, people won't do what's necessary to accomplish success.

Second, *success demands personal targets*. People can't succeed by aiming at someone else's targets, although it's possible to begin the journey of success that way. Without passion, people won't do what's necessary to accomplish success.

Third, *success happens today and every day, not tomorrow or someday*. The only time you can be successful is *now*. You can laugh, love, act, or solve a problem, *now*. People who live only in the future are just as unhappy as those who live only in the past.

Once you set up some general parameters to define success, you can then get specific so that the definition applies only to you, your business, and your life. In the process, you will establish a target for your life. It may change from time to time, but it will always encapsulate the meaning of success to you personally. This becomes a lifelong target, or a mission.

At the beginning of this book I told you my mission: To help people get into their own businesses and to teach them the system for success that I follow so that they can lead happy lives.

As I accomplish my mission, working at it every day, I achieve success. The mission constantly gives new meaning to my life, motivating me, energizing me. Because of that mission, I feel things that someone without a mission would never experience. I hear an inner voice that speaks to me constantly, keeping me on course, guiding me toward the completion of my mission, a lifetime of work. I live every day as if it were my only day. I am happy with every experience, enjoying every moment with the people I love. My philosophy is as follows: Take care of today and tomorrow will take care of itself.

You, too, need a mission statement. Not only will it provide guidance, it will make your life more exciting, because the pursuit of any mission demands peak performance. You'll learn to become more efficient, to hit your target dreams faster. You will automatically attract other people who will want to join you, interlocking their mission with your mission. And you will stay the course, realizing that happiness is the process of achieving the mission—not the mission itself.

What's standing in the way of your living, leading, reaching that elusive state of happiness? Nothing but conditioning. If you recall, that's where this book began. That's where it also concludes.

It is my hope that this book has helped you move closer to starting your own business, to using a system that

I know from experience will provide fulfillment and happiness in your life.

Peace and Plenty!

ACTION ITEM

You know that line, "Today is the first day of the rest of my life?" Change it for this exercise to say, "Today is the last day of the rest of my life." Morbid, I know, but drama frequently creates change.

Pretend that you died. And pretend that you consciously attended your own funeral, where someone you loved read your eulogy.

What would you hope the eulogy would say?

Think about that. Then, write the eulogy. Yes, write your own eulogy.

When you read the eulogy back to yourself, it will surely reflect the values and qualities of the person you most want to be. Would you be able to say the eulogy accurately describes you? Today?

If not, what must you do differently to deserve that eulogy?

Your answers will help you form short and long-term targets. Start aiming at them every day!

In the words of Emerson, "Make the most of yourself, for that is all there is of you."

For Additional Information

Want to know more about Don Dwyer's system of success?
Have a question you want to ask Don Dwyer about getting
into your own business, or about franchising? **For a list of
franchisors who will assist you with financing up to 50%
of their franchise fee, call, write, or fax Don Dwyer:**

The Dwyer Group
P.O. Box 3146
Waco, Texas 76707
Telephone: 817-756-2122
Fax: 817-753-2909